ELECTRIC BOATS

ELECTRIC BOATS

THE HANDBOOK OF
CLEAN, QUIET BOATING

DOUGLAS LITTLE

INTERNATIONAL MARINE
CAMDEN, MAINE

Published by International Marine®

10   9   8   7   6   5   4   3   2

Copyright © 1994 International Marine®, an imprint of TAB Books. TAB Books is a division of McGraw-Hill, Inc.

Library of Congress Cataloging-in-Publication Data
Little, Douglas.
      Electric Boats : the handbook of clean, quiet boating. / Douglas Little.
          p. cm.
     Includes index.
     ISBN 0-07-038104-6 (alk. paper)
      1. Electric Boats. I. Title.
   VM345.L57 1993
   623.8'231--dc20   93-39535
                                              CIP

Questions regarding the content of this book should be addressed to:
International Marine
P.O. Box 220
Camden, ME 04843
Questions regarding the ordering of this book should be addressed to:
TAB Books
A Division of McGraw-Hill, Inc.
Blue Ridge Summit, PA 17294
1-800-233-1128

 Electric Boats is printed on 60-pound Renew Opaque Vellum, an acid-free paper that contains 50 percent recycled waste paper (preconsumer) and 10 percent postconsumer waste paper.

Printed by Fairfield Arcata, Fairfield, Pennsylvania
Design by Ann Aspell
Illustrations by Benjamin L. White
Production by Molly Mulhern
Edited by Jim Babb, Don Casey, and Paula Blanchard

CONTENTS

ACKNOWLEDGMENTS

I THANK MY WIFE, SANDY, for her contributions to this book and our boats. I am indebted to all the electric-boat builders who provided information about their boats for this book, to Richard Lebovitz for his contribution of material, and to Dave Gerr for formulas from the *Propeller Handbook*. I want also to recognize the following persons for their contributions: Irvin G. Clator, Ph.D.–Physics, University of North Carolina, Wilmington, for his assistance in building *Najas*; Mike Alford, Curator of Maritime Research, North Carolina Maritime Museum, for his drawings and ideas, and Rodney Barfield, Director, for his support; and Leslie Helms for her help in photography and evaluation.

INTRODUCTION

IN THE FOLLOWING PAGES the reader is likely to find more the ramblings of a boatbuilder than the measured words of an author; just as likely to read of river trips and the hazards of backwater exploring as of the boats that make it possible. For me, time on the river is time in Nature's classroom, where the boat and its occupants are at one with Nature. New ideas need the kind of consistent evaluation that comes only through application, and the lessons thus learned are important ones: how to produce craft that are in harmony both with their occupants' expectations and with the environment in which they operate.

Electric propulsion in itself is not complex. Electric boats can vary quite a bit in size, but this is usually just a matter of scale—a large electric boat behaves in a similar manner to a smaller one. Their greatest differences are likely to be their operating environments. This book acquaints the reader with tools and ideas to use in thinking out an electric dreamboat. Whether that boat is a 30-foot launch or an electric canoe, the essential information presented here applies equally. My objective has been to touch on many subjects, leaving the reader open to follow the avenues of his or her particular interest.

By the time I finished writing this book, I had learned a lot more about electric boats than I knew when I started. I invite you to come along now and share in this learning experience.

CHAPTER 1

AN AFTERNOON ON THE RIVER

IT IS A BEAUTIFUL DAY, the first to indicate that the better part of summer is over. The air is crisp and clear, the trees showing hints of color that will later blossom into fall. It is an excellent afternoon to be in a boat on the river.

I finish up those things that will set the afternoon free, casting longing glances in the direction of the fine-lined little boat that will make the day complete. With loose ends tied up and the boat secure on the truck—its cooler iced, the vest and paddle stowed—the first feelings of harmony set in. I check my bag, map and compass, camera and field glasses. All is there. My float plan is posted, and with a kiss from the wife and closing words to the children, I'm off the few land miles to the riverbank to enjoy the afternoon in my electric boat.

THE OUTING

The Black River Guide, or more simply the Guide, is the appropriate craft for this afternoon's outing. At 85 pounds the Guide is not light, but I prefer to carry it to the river's edge rather than drag it. The footing is good, and with relative ease the Guide slips into the dark water and glides the length of its tether. There is the familiar gurgle of water filling the prop cavity as I pull the craft to its best beach. Back to the truck now to lock it up and borrow its battery.

There is much to be said for this 60-pound fellow traveler. For one thing, as long as it is in the truck's battery box, it is usually charged. Today's decision to use the deep-cycle marine (DCM) battery in the truck is a well-thought-out and, for me, relatively common practice. When it has served this day's work, the truck will give it a recharge for almost nothing. All things secure on the hill, the lead-acid man in my hand, we are ready.

The Black River Guide. Its low profile, shallow draft, and good speed make it a good choice for a one-person outing.

The stretch of river chosen today is reasonably clear of obstacles and close to home, and though I have been here many times, its tranquillity has not been diminished. I map my power usage to leave enough energy to start the truck when I return: downriver at 5 amps for 4 hours then 1 hour upstream at 20 amps, or a total of about 40 amp-hours (Ah)—a reasonable expectation from a 105-Ah deep-cycle battery. With field glasses at hand, map and compass before me, and hand on the tiller, I am off for a slow cruise down the river.

The Guide is bone dry, its varnished walnut and juniper glistening in the autumn sun. I am running about 5 amps by the gauge, stepping up when necessary to avoid snags or to make quick turns, and sometimes cutting back and just drifting in the broad water. The motor is running free, and I can hear the change in its small hum as the prop loads in the slow current of the deep, still bends.

The river is relatively low, its speed in the narrows less than a knot, about the same as my boatspeed. There will be shallows of less than 6 inches, and I need to stay in the channel. Ahead I see the glimmer of light on the water's rippled surface, probably a submerged log across the river bed. I hold a steady speed to cross at the deepest water. When the log is directly under the boat, I see there is a sufficient 8 inches, and the skeg clears a second later without a bump. In areas with ample current, it is easy to read what might be just below the water's surface, but the calm waters of the bends yield little information except that it's slow and probably deep. Sleepers, as I call them—old logs or large pieces of debris extending from the river bottom to just beneath the surface, camouflaged and masked by the dark water of the river—lie in wait there to trip the unwary boater.

Farther ahead the light from the ripples is disorienting and I miss the channel. The skeg drags, skipping on the ripples of the sand in the shallows, and I slide forward a foot or so to get the stern up and reduce draft. Once back in the channel, I make a note of this place so it will not be a problem on the trip back upriver.

One of the most enjoyable experiences on the river is making the judgment calls necessary to avoid snags or fallen trees, especially when a 3-knot freshet is pulling the boat along. A fallen tree covering most of the passage may have shallow branches to run over, but the Guide's skeg easily protects the prop. Depth is usually not the problem when passing under the trunk of a toppled tree, but head clearance sometimes is. Lying down in the Guide lets you clear most anything over 14 inches above the water, but remember to remove your hat. While the quick decisions needed in running a freshet can be exciting, they won't be necessary today as the river is slow and easy.

I have been a frequent traveler on this river for many years and have lived and worked on its bank for most of them. Once I left our shop and took the river's course to the sea. It took five days in a canoe, a most educating experience, one largely responsible for the design of our boats. Large outboards or big boats can be used on only a small portion of this river, mostly near the coast. The canoe, pirogue, and kayak, however, are quite at home for almost all of its length. The electric Guide has evolved to complement the accommodations the river has to offer, and though it does not replace the reliable canoe, it is an alternative to it.

Wildlife sightings this day are numerous. Several hawks are about most of the trip. Field glasses are not needed to see the deer watching from the riverbank as the Guide slips silently downstream. Later, a beaver, an otter, and many ducks appear, some within camera range, but today I just observe.

Too soon 4 hours are up. I am at a large, deep bend in the river shown on the map; someone is usually fishing here, but today I have the river to myself. These are familiar waters, but I practice locating myself with map and compass to hone my skills for future trips to new waters. As the Guide slips onto the white sandy beach opposite the high bank of the bend, I think it might have been a good idea to have brought fishing gear. No. I would rather just mess about with the boat. A walk about and a snack and it's underway again.

Traveling upstream, the Guide can really show its stuff. An electric boat has opened many areas to me that were impractical in my old canoe. Now I can take the Guide on short notice to almost any place I wish to see, spend a day or an afternoon going upstream or down, and be confident of making it back to the hill. While

AN AFTERNOON ON THE RIVER

canoe trips are usually downstream, typically requiring a vehicle or someone to meet you at the take-out, the electric Guide gives me independence from this awkward situation and the freedom to do mostly as I wish on the river. Because of this freedom and the easy nature of this little electric craft, I have traveled to more places and seen more wildlife and vegetation than I could have had the canoe been my only water transportation. The Guide's electric power has made the difference, yet among canoeists in the swamps and on the river, the boat is not out of place—just an evolutionary step. The Guide is now my boat of choice.

The Guide is making good speed running up the river. Playing about is fun—seeing how close to a tree or a snag you can go and still make it. Going faster leaves less reaction time; this is when the sleepers can really trip you up. Wildlife sightings are still common as, even at this speed, the boat is relatively quiet, the greatest noise coming from the wake on a shallow beach. It seems hardly any time until the truck is in view.

Reluctant to return, I run upriver a bit and play about with the boat. As the light fades, I am on the hill with the battery in hand. In only minutes I'll know if the power plan was correct. The truck fires after a few turns. Back to the water for the Guide and then home. As I put the boat back in its shelter and wipe it down, I wonder: How can anything be nicer than an afternoon on the river in a good electric boat?

THE CASE

Electric watercraft have a definite place and purpose. Sure, there are other boats that could do some of the same things, but could they encompass as many? A canoe, for example, is almost silent under paddle—if you are an experienced paddler and don't bump the boat or splash the water. But paddling the canoe leaves no hands free for field glasses or a camera. Not so with the Guide or other appropriate electric craft. Moving upstream while lying in a boat to clear a 14-inch-above-water tree trunk, you cannot paddle and therefore cannot make forward progress. The precise control of a good electric boat is one of its best characteristics. In its typical quiet manner, it carries out what is asked of it with a precision that a paddler may work years to achieve. A paddler does have the distinct advantage that his craft can go as far and for as long as he is willing to paddle.

An *advantage* of electric-powered craft most often overlooked is the absence of high speed. Electric boats generally have displacement hulls and operate at relatively low speeds, usually under 5 knots. Once while boating with a friend on *his* river in an electric boat, he was constantly bringing to my attention flora on the riverbank he had never noticed before, yet he spent a great deal of time in his gas-powered boat on this same stretch of water. It was our conclusion that in the faster boat, there was no way to notice, no time to see the flowers. The reduction of speed and absence of water noises of the gas outboard make for an entirely different outing.

All this is not to imply electric boats are slow; by canoe, kayak, or small sailboat standards they are not. That 60-pound lead-acid man you carry with you in the Guide is good for all day at a canoe's pace, with a shorter-term ability to leave most paddle traffic far behind. I have seen times, in the shallow and obstacle-filled environment of the upper river, when the electric Guide could keep up with a gas outboard.

The primary limitations of electric boats are usually associated with energy reserves, but even this can be overcome.

Our work with electric boats did not create a craft like the Guide without consideration for how it was to be used. The concept of any boat requires careful consideration of many factors.

THE DEFINITION

An electric boat can be as simple as an electric trolling motor on a canoe or as complex as a 50-mph speedboat. This book concerns *only* boats using electricity as their *prime* propulsion source. A 150-horsepower (h.p.) bass boat with a 50-pound-thrust, 24-volt trolling motor is not an electric boat. An aluminum jonboat designed to plane with a 15-h.p. outboard but sometimes powered by a submersible electric motor is not an electric boat. A sailboat with an electric auxiliary, though its easily driven displacement hull lends good characteristics for electric propulsion, is not an electric boat.

An electric boat is one that uses an electric motor as its primary means of propulsion. The motor might be inboard with a hull-piercing shaft and a conventional three-blade prop, it could be an inboard-outboard configuration, or it can be just an outboard. This is not to say that there are not many boats that are adaptable to electric power: pirogues, canoes, kayaks, pontoon boats, traditional launches, and other displacement boats are good candidates for electric propulsion. On our river, for example, most of the small, one-man pirogues have been progressively altered to be completely electric. Not that they can no longer be paddled, for they can, but not as effectively or through the range given them by their modified trolling motors. The degree of control gained through electric propulsion is such that the short paddle rarely goes in the water. They are no longer pirogues; they are electric boats or electric canoes. If this point is not taken to heart, be prepared to pay the fines for improper registration.

Electric boats have simple requirements. Along with a good hull, you need an energy source, a power control system, and an electric motor. What sets an *electric boat* apart from an *electric-powered boat* is the degree to which these components are incorporated into the design; in an electric boat they are not add-ons or modifications. A functional and simple electric-boat design would include battery placement for maximum stability and concealment, speed and steering control in the tiller handle, and comfortable seating. A battery is a very simple device, as is the electric motor; there is no need for an electric boat to be complex.

The most significant drawback on any electric boat is its limited capacity to store electrical energy. We will look at various methods to replenish electrical consumption while underway, at rest, or dockside. The potential for "free" energy from photovoltaics will be examined. Taking a cue from locomotives that use electric motors to propel the train and petro-powered generators to drive the electric motors, we will consider the use of a similar hybrid system for electric propulsion on the water.

The electric boat Najas *demonstrates how components such as motor, batteries, and controls are a part of a true electric boat, not added on.*

The rear compartment of Najas *holds a generator that can easily be removed as well as operated on board. The battery is located in the bow.*

This book is meant to be the first word in electric boats but certainly not the last. Doubtless I have overlooked some items, said perhaps too much about others, but most of what follows comes from a mind that would rather be on the river in an electric boat than write about it. Of course, the choice of an electric boat reflects ideas about environment and the way pleasure is taken that lend themselves to that way of thinking. Ahead are some facts, opinions, speculations, and ideas associated with electric boats. Try not to take them too seriously—or too lightly. Electric propulsion will not replace most other means of powering boats on the water today, nor is it the purpose of this book to suggest mass conversions or to imply that all powered watercraft should be electric.

On the river this afternoon, my thoughts had turned, as usual, to the next boat I might build—dreaming with my eyes wide open. This stretch of river was the upper limit of steamboat travel at the turn of the century. Downstream, about an hour away, lies the remains of the old riverboat that once brought commerce to this area. It would be great, I think, to build an electric boat that could carry four people or so along the same route that old ship took—a boat drawing a foot at most, and narrow enough to squeeze between the snags. I could be captain of my own ship, carrying paying passengers. Then, rounding a bend in the river, I find that the left bank has been clear-cut as far as the eye can see. The bubble pops. Who would ever want to see this, let alone pay for the trip? With hand clinched on the tiller and a blind eye to the riverbank, I start again. Maybe a small boat for just two, one that is rugged and can get far enough into the swamps to miss this carnage. Yes, I think, and the dream again begins to take shape.

An electric boat with everything necessary for an outing on board—including room for a companion.

Most everyone has a dreamboat. May some of them be electric.

AN AFTERNOON ON THE RIVER

CHAPTER 2

BOATING AND THE ENVIRONMENT

ON MY SLOW, DARKWATER RIVER—typical of the southern coastal plain—where navigating the shallow water and dodging snags and sleepers are common practices, the fossil-fuel outboard is neither prevalent nor always practical. Closer to the coast, where the water is larger, this is no longer true. Even when these craft aren't in sight, your senses tell you they use the water. The odor of marsh gases and vegetation is replaced by the smell of the two-cycle outboard, a smell that takes me back to my boyhood and fishing with my Uncle George, but now, that is the *only* pleasant sensation revived. Floating oil slicks, especially near landings and docks, diffract rainbow colors and meander to disperse along the banks. Where vegetation is present, it is soiled and coated, unable to shed this unwanted cloak in a cleansing summer rain. Much of the bank is denuded by the wakes of boats pushed by these powerful motors; other stretches are eroded under the canopy of vegetation, introducing more plants to the rigors of life with pollutants.

GASOLINE ENGINES

The high power-to-weight ratio of the two-cycle gasoline engine makes it the ideal power plant for many small, portable machines—such devices as chain saws, leaf blowers, motorbikes, and of course, marine outboards. It is the engine's simplicity of design that gives it such versatility and appeal—and causes its unclean operating characteristics. To understand why the two-cycle engine is such an offender compared with the four-cycle engine, one needs only a simple understanding of the two.

A four-cycle engine operates in four distinct steps or cycles. On the piston's first down-stroke, the fuel-air mixture is drawn into the cylinder through an open intake valve. With the intake valve closed, the up-stroke of the piston compresses the gases. At the top of the compression stroke, the fuel is ignited, driving the piston back down in the power-stroke. The gases inside the cylinder, tightly contained during these three strokes, are exhausted through an open exhaust valve by the fourth and final up-stroke. It is the positive containment and complete combustion of the fuel that make the four-cycle engine distinctly different from the two-stroke engine.

Instead of valves, two-cycle engines have ports—slots or openings in the base of the cylinder wall. The fuel-air mixture is delivered to the cylinder by way of the crankcase, compressed there by the piston's down-stroke. When the piston is at its lowest position, the ports uncover and the pressurized fuel-air mix enters the cylinder. Because both the exhaust and intake ports are open at the same time, some raw fuel exits the exhaust port. The up-stroke closes the ports and compresses the fuel charge. The ignited fuel drives the piston back down, opening the exhaust port to expel the exhaust gases and opening the intake port for the next fuel charge, and the cycle repeats itself. The reality of this design—that both ports are open during the intake of fuel—dooms this simple machine to unclean operation; that, and the fact that the oil mixed with the gasoline, required for lubrication, is expelled mostly unchanged in the exhaust gases. Alternatives to the two-cycle outboard are the cleaner-burning four-cycle engine—outboard, inboard, or stern drive—or electric propulsion. Were pollution the only issue, the four-cycle engine would be the superior choice for most watercraft. Even though electric craft can be up to 100 percent nonpolluting, electric propulsion is not practical for most watercraft using outboards. Electric craft are best suited by their relatively low power-to-weight ratio to use in a small, closed, and quiet environment. They are not in themselves a solution to the evils of pollution, but they are a most appropriate alternative for the many applications where environmental issues play a larger role than traversing large open areas of water at high speeds.

If troubling statistics could universally impact attitudes about pollution, a much greater change would already have taken place. Unfortunately the isolation of a problem through numbers tends to take it from the real world and pass it to some higher power for a solution. And as impressive as the numbers can be, they often misrepresent the problem in their smallness of concentration. Not that we should altogether disregard the statistics, but the unpleasantness of following a two-cycle outboard on a close and quiet stream cannot be expressed statistically. Clearing a fouled prop of fishing line or stepping on broken glass on what was once clean, white beach are real events, easily understood. A river reduced to a ditch by clear-cutting is expressed by the number of degrees the water temperature may rise, not the fact that an ecosystem has been destroyed. As antiquated as it might seem, the truth still lies in what one can see, smell, taste, touch, and experience firsthand.

Meanwhile, warring factions hurl statistics back and forth like mortar rounds, hoping with each barrage to strike a target that is nothing more than the previous set of numbers. In this battle between greed and conservation, between ignorance and awareness, opposing sides inflate and deflate the numbers like a body count in an effort to show their side right or winning, while all of Nature's creatures continue to lose.

Yet, there are some compelling statistics. Andre Mele, in his startling *Polluting for Pleasure* (W. W. Norton, 1993), tells us that the two-cycle outboard emits 140 times more pollutants, horsepower-for-horsepower, than the automobile. In the same book we see the disparity between industry statistics for annual two-cycle pollution—133 million gallons—and those from environmentalists—400 million gallons. So we can choose to believe that two-cycle outboards pump 40 times more oil into the water annually than spilled from the Exxon *Valdez*, or *only* 13 times the *Valdez* spill. Such numbers are clearly horrifying indictments of the technical realities of a simple machine made and used for a particular purpose, but *it is you or me who fills the tank and turns the key.*

As the environment continues to suffer from the effects of burning fossil fuel, much is being said, but efforts to reduce this consumption are limited to a few small initiatives by relatively small groups of individuals. The lion's share of fossil-fuel-related pollution comes from automobiles, making the electric alternative a sought-after prize as possibly a major solution. Much of this leading-edge technology for electrical land vehicles could be directly turned toward use in electric watercraft, and in many ways electric boats offer greater promise because of their inherent slow speed and their capacity to carry a larger resource of stored energy.

The significant distinction between the electric land vehicle and the electric boat, other than the surface they travel, is their use. It would be fair to say that most watercraft, particularly those in the size range we are considering for electric propulsion, are used for recreation—not the case for the electric car. When it comes to recreation and that precious time off, dollars become secondary and the environmental impact is not likely to get any consideration at all. Spending several hundred dollars to supply gasoline and oil to a pair of 200-h.p. two-cycle outboards is shrugged off as money well spent on a good time—damn the environment and full speed ahead. It is our attitudes, not our machines, that threaten our environment. Thus electric boats are not likely to become a true commodity in the market until they are mandated by laws and restrictions. There are always those who are ahead of the masses, however, and can appreciate the value of electric propulsion without having to be told.

ELECTRIC POWER

Utility companies have a lot of experience efficiently producing electricity from fossil fuel. To some degree other sources—nuclear, hydro, solar, and wind—contribute to the power grid. We can safely assume that a large and closely regulated utility is less of a polluter, pound for pound of fossil fuel consumed, than a two-cycle outboard. According to the U.S. Department of Energy, today's low-emission automobiles produce 200 times more pollution than generating the electricity to propel an electric vehicle the same distance, and we have already seen that the two-cycle outboard is 140 times more polluting than the automobile. So even if our battery bank is replenished from a fossil-fuel power grid, the percentage of resulting pollutants will certainly be less. (The core remains from nuclear power might be another story.)

Excepting nuclear generation, virtually all our electric power is derived from the sun, either from the past as coal, oil, or natural gas, or in the present as hydro, wind, solar (*photovoltaics*). (Minor exceptions to this rule are power produced through tidal flows and geothermal activity.) Heat and combustion by-products resulting from the consumption of fossil fuels and the rapid depletion of deposits that took eons to accrete cannot help but disrupt the present natural order. Our most friendly power sources are the present ones, and of those, photovoltaic comes to mind as the most direct conversion into electricity with the least consequence to our environment. Hydroelectric plants dam strong rivers, create lakes, and alter the natural course of events—they change things. Biomass, or wood, though naturally efficient in translating solar power to fuel value, is more important as a guardian of our atmosphere, refreshing the air and cleaning it of toxins already in overabundance. The only pollution from windmills is a bit of noise (and bird mortalities), but they require a strong and consistent breezeway. The by-product of photovoltaics is pure unadulterated shade—the perfect roof for a carport or boathouse. This power source combined with electric propulsion would yield the cleanest and most environmentally friendly powered watercraft.

The power to replenish the battery of my electric boat usually comes from the local power grid, which is 30 percent nuclear and 70 percent fossil fuel, or from the incidental output of my truck alternator. While this power is not the cleanest, it is the most practical at this time—cleaner and kinder to the environment by far than equivalent two-cycle gasoline power. When the particulars of emission are fully considered, there are many ways to pick apart the issue of pollution, some of which are not easy to comprehend. Though these are of great importance, the more obvious effects should be enough to warrant thoughts of cleaner, less disruptive means of traversing our precious water. If the care for the environment is present, the rest will fall in place naturally.

ENVIRONMENTAL REALITIES

Whether we believe the EPA statistics cited by Andre Mele in *Polluting for Pleasure,* claiming that each year gas outboards pump *40 times more* oil into our waters than was spilled into the pristine waters off Alaska by the Exxon *Valdez;* or whether we believe industry statistics supplied by two major American outboard manufacturers claiming a mere 13 times the *Valdez* spill, how can anyone fail to be impressed by the suggestion of a routine annual "spill" even 5 times greater? Even if the industry statistic is closer to the truth, it still brings home the point that sometimes destruction can be just as devastating in small and quiet increments. We should not assume that Nature's waters can handle any pollution we can put into it, as long as it's in small enough doses. As with camping or hiking, if you take it with you then keep it with you; don't leaving *anything* behind.

Not only do boats affect the environment, but the environment affects boating as well. Nature is most often the reason the electric boater is on the water at all. If the environment is altered to the point where there is nothing one wants to see, hear, smell, or feel on the water, then why need a boat to begin with?

For years I have studied the Venus's-flytrap and other carnivorous plants indigenous to this area. I am also on the lookout for fallen Atlantic white cedar for boat-building—*I do not harvest living trees.* Today the carnivorous plants are rarer and almost all the cedar is standing or lying dead because of changes in the environment. The Forest Service requests seed for replanting the rapidly fading cedar, and there are penalties for taking carnivorous plants from the wild. Good intentions? Sure, but they mean absolutely nothing if the fragile environment necessary for the plants is not protected, and it isn't. Each day waste from agricultural operations flows into some previously pristine sphagnum environment, effectively signing its death warrant. And every day development nibbles away at our dwindling wetlands.

Two days downriver are some of the oldest trees east of the Rockies. Naturalists and river travelers come from great distances to see these noble cypress trees and their habitat. This is the realm of the electric canoe, the kind of environment that evokes a reverence of Nature. Without these trees, there is no need for the boat. The beauty of all our rivers and streams lies in the trees along their banks and the animals for which the trees provide sanctuary.

A river without its trees is a ditch, and few people, including me, have any desire to go boating in a ditch. Yet it seems that every few months surveyors' markers appear in a different place on the riverbank, and, as predictable as death itself, in my next passing the bank will be bare. Leftover limbs and trees, downed but not taken, litter the river's edge. "They grow back" is a bankrupt argument for this action: big trees that are lost will not be seen again even in the lifetime of my children. Who can fail to see that even a narrow margin of 100 feet or so of woods along a riverbank is of much greater value left alone than taken for money? These mature trees stabilize the riverbank, provide habitats for wildlife, and are so very beautiful. It is a lesson we should all learn.

Our rivers and swamps are filters that clean and refresh the waters. They cannot do this if destroyed or overburdened with pollutants. Awareness of these problems and understanding the importance of the wetlands environment are essential for the sake of our children.

CHOICES

You are probably asking yourself, "What has all this to do with an electric boat?" Everything. It is about attitudes, personal choices, and compromise. We all need to understand that we impact our environment in every aspect of our daily existence, and we all choose the extent of that impact. The electric boat represents a choice between quiet observation, reflection, and serenity and the uncaring, opportunistic, and selfish use of our waterways.

The slow-moving manatee is endangered in America, killed and maimed with alarming regularity by gasoline-powered runabouts. It is unlikely that one of these gentle giants has ever been injured by an electric boat. An unjust comparison, you say. Perhaps. It is true that the sheer number of powerboats compared with electric craft is overwhelming, and the modest speed and limited miles covered reduce even more the chance of a collision between an electric boat and a manatee. It is the *choice* of the electric boater, however, that makes the difference—not so much the choice of craft but the choice of purpose in boating. The electric boater chooses not to pull a skier, not to use 150 h.p. to get that record bass to the weigh station. No flying spray in the face. No roar of a high-powered engine. He or she is not in a hurry, not going too fast to see what is all around—out, in fact, to appreciate the environment. The pleasure is in the quiet and comfort afforded by the craft, the almost reverential whispered conversations with companions, and the mosaic of curious observations on the outing, which may well include the sighting of a manatee and will not include the telltale iridescent sheen of an oil-saturated exhaust emanating from our—and there's no other word—*pleasure* craft.

Choices. Choices based on attitudes and lifestyles. Choices between serene and sensational, between observation and blur. Not so much a compromise as a matter of choice. Some choose the canoe and kayak for all these reasons plus the vigor of exercise and independence. Some choose to sail, harnessing their fate to the wind. The electric boat has its own appeal, offering precision of control, quiet operation, and minimal impact on the environment. Present-day electric craft are not for everyone, though as time passes and attitudes change, more and more they may become a clean, quiet alternative.

CHAPTER 3

ENERGY BASICS AND ELECTRIC PROPULSION

THERE ARE MANY WAYS TO MOVE A BOAT THROUGH THE WATER:
sail in its many configurations (including the kite for pulling kayaks), the paddle,
the pole, and probably the oldest and most universal, the oar. Even animals harnessed
to tow lines are still used to pull canal barges and rafts in some parts of the world, and
given man's inventiveness, numerous other means undoubtedly exist.

The steam engine ushered in a new era in watercraft propulsion, at first rotating a paddle wheel, then later spinning a propeller. The propeller continues to be the
most common means of power transmission, but steam has been replaced by gasoline or diesel—and to a lesser degree by electricity. Electric systems are selected
when they are the most appropriate for the application. Their characteristics include
reliability, low maintenance, quiet operation, and the ability to function in a closed
environment.

Overcoming the resistance of water to move a boat is a manner of using energy
to do work. The wind is solar and it's free. Sailors might wish to carry a 20-knot
breeze in the locker, but this is an energy source external to the craft. So are tow
lines, currents, and tides. For a craft to be "self-propelled," the energy must be
taken aboard, enough for the duration of the voyage. How much and what type of
stored energy must be carried depend on the type, size, speed, and operating environment of the craft. Old steamers burned a lot of wood or coal through fairly
inefficient energy systems. The development of liquid fossil fuels allowed for com-
pact storage of a high-energy substance. This is the most significant difference

between electric propulsion and engines using fossil fuels. If only we could tank up on electricity like gasoline.

Energy storage should be the first consideration in the use of electric propulsion. Electricity has no mass; it is mostly pure energy. Unfortunately, when electrical energy is stored rather than generated using another energy source, the storage container is relatively massive and weighs the same, full or empty. Whereas a fuel tank for liquid fossil fuel is relatively light when empty, the electric storage tank is not. We had best recognize this apparent negative and plan now to turn it into an advantage.

Impressive amounts of ballast—stone, iron, lead, or whatever—are added to some boats to provide adequate stability. Here is a design requirement that could make good use of the mass of a battery bank. But the fact that such heavily ballasted boats tend to remain in the water reminds us again of the light weight and ease in overland transportation of boats using fossil-fuel engines. As with all design work, there are compromises. Let's begin by looking at what we want and what is practical.

The use of electricity as the energy source for primary propulsion requires either generation or storage. Concurrent onboard generation of electricity using fossil fuel is not nearly as efficient as using the fuel to power the propulsion system directly, so we are likely to need a means of storing electrical power—the storage battery. It would be easy to get bogged down with the particulars of relating electrical to mechanical power, especially weights, storage capacities, and the other details required to fully understand various energy systems. Instead, we will keep it simple. Specific conversions can be obtained from the various suppliers' literature or almost any handbook, such as *12-Volt Bible for Boats* by Miner Brotherton (International Marine, 1985).

ELECTRICITY

A common and effective analogy drawn between electricity and water may well be helpful when speaking of the electric boat. Fill a cylinder with water and the water exerts a force on the walls of the vessel. The taller the column of water, the greater the force exerted on the container and the greater the potential of the water to do work. *Work* is defined as moving a mass against an opposing force—such as gravity or friction. Until movement takes place, no work is being done. In the cylinder we have a tall column of water of a specific mass, and by opening the valve we can give this mass an opportunity to do work. This is *potential,* and in electrical terms it is equivalent to voltage, or *electrical potential*, which is measured in *volts*. The taller the column of water, the greater the voltage.

A tall, thin column of water has the same potential as a column of water of equal height in a cylinder of a greater diameter. The amount of work that can be done, however, is related to the mass as well as the potential. As the larger-diameter cylinder contains more mass, or water, it can do more work upon opening the valve. This flow can be described as *current*. Electrical current is most often expressed in *amperes*. Amperes, or amps, represent the volume of flow, whereas volts represent the potential at which this volume is held.

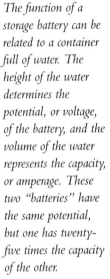

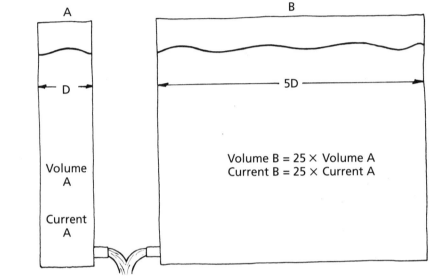

The function of a storage battery can be related to a container full of water. The height of the water determines the potential, or voltage, of the battery, and the volume of the water represents the capacity, or amperage. These two "batteries" have the same potential, but one has twenty-five times the capacity of the other.

BATTERIES

We will later explore in greater detail the subject of batteries for use in electric watercraft; for now, let's touch on the basics. In many respects the battery for watercraft propulsion resembles the typical automobile battery. It may be indistinguishable

A rather ordinary 12-volt, 105-Ah deep-cycle open-cell lead-acid battery. This particular battery is over two years old and has lost some of its capacity to hard use and deep discharges. The carrying strap is a very important part of any battery that is removed regularly from the boat.

from the *deep-cycle* battery used for golf carts or trolling motors. For easy reference, let's consider a rather ordinary 12-volt lead-acid deep-cycle battery of 100-Ah capacity. We will refer to this throughout the book as our standard battery, not to imply that it is the most commonly used or the battery of choice, but just to provide a fixed reference in our discussions of the various components.

There is much to be said about batteries. Types and sizes are numerous and often misleading and confusing. Amp-hour ratings may vary depending on application, but they are generally determined by the battery's ability to deliver a particular current over a particular period of time—usually 20 hours in the U.S. In the case of our standard 100-Ah battery, this would be 5 amps over 20 hours.

$$5 \text{ amps} \times 20 \text{ hours} = 100 \text{ amp-hours}$$

Any greater current draw than 5 amps would reduce the amp-hour value. For example, this battery might supply 40 amps for only 1 hour, or 30 amps for 2 hours. The smaller the draw or the larger the battery bank, the more efficient the system. In Chapter 6 we will discuss at length the many factors that affect battery performance. Meanwhile, since most 12-volt deep-cycle batteries can be rated above 100 Ah, we will assume for now that our standard battery is rated at 25 amps; i.e., that it is capable of supplying a current of 25 amps for a period of 4 hours.

$$25 \text{ amps} \times 4 \text{ hours} = 100 \text{ amp-hours}$$

We have defined our sample battery this way for simplicity; the fact is, most batteries rated at 100 Ah won't actually deliver a 25-amp current for much longer than 2 hours. In later chapters we will examine the various factors that determine *actual* capacity. It is important to note that few electric boats are always operated at top speed, and doing so greatly reduces overall efficiency. A balanced battery bank providing maximum power when needed and maximum efficiency for normal use is described in Chapter 7.

Though weights vary with construction and capacity, most batteries similar to our hypothetical standard weigh around 60 pounds and measure about 7 inches × 9 inches × 13 inches, or 0.47 cubic feet.

$$7 \text{ inches} \times 9 \text{ inches} \times 13 \text{ inches} = 819 \text{ cubic inches}$$
$$819 \text{ cubic inches}/1{,}728 \text{ cubic inches per cubic foot} = 0.47 \text{ cubic feet}$$

POWER

Power is the capacity to do work. Let's return to the water analogy to understand electric power. Thousands of gallons of water flow past a given point in my river every minute, but because here in the southern coastal plains the drop in the water level is gradual, the height—*head* in hydro-electrical terms—is not great. So, much to my dismay, the generation of power is not feasible; the potential of the large current is too small to overcome the resistance of a water-driven generator. On the other hand, someone in the mountains might use the lesser 25-gallon-per-minute flow of a small stream, but with 20 feet of head, to produce 1,000 watt-hours (Wh) (41.67 watts per hour x 24 hours) per day of electricity. Both current and potential are required to do work. In electrical terms we can express this as:

$$P = V \times A$$
where
P = power in watt
V = potential in volts
and
A = current in amps

Using this formula, we can calculate the power available from our standard battery as 1,200 Wh.

$$100 \text{ amp-hours} \times 12 \text{ volts} = 1,200 \text{ watt-hours}$$

Because we used capacity (in amp-hours) rather than current (in amps), our answer must be expressed in watt-hours. Technically, this is a measurement of energy used over time rather than power, but we need not concern ourselves with this distinction, except to note that when A is in amp-hours, P will be in watt-hours.

From this we can calculate the energy density of our sample battery:

$$1,200 \text{ watt-hours}/60 \text{ pounds} = 20 \text{ watt-hours per pound}$$

To sum up, we have a 100-Ah-capacity 12-volt battery to be used at a 25-amp rate, delivering a total of 1,200 Wh. At a weight of 60 pounds, that gives us an energy density of 20 Wh per pound.

These numbers reflect a total discharge, and we will see in later chapters that it is neither common nor good practice to discharge a battery completely. Offsetting this limitation somewhat is the fact that electric boats are usually not operated at full power for long periods. The numbers above are accurate only to a point and should be used as a guide and not the gospel.

In relating mechanical power in horsepower to electrical power in watts, we will use 1 h.p. = 750 watts, which is close enough to the exact value (of 746 watts) for our purpose. A 12-volt motor drawing 25 amps is rated at 300 watts, equal to about 0.4 h.p.

$$25 \text{ amps} \times 12 \text{ volts} = 300 \text{ watts}$$
$$300 \text{ watts} \times 1 \text{ horsepower}/750 \text{ watts} = 0.4 \text{ horsepower}$$

Most electric motors in this power range used in marine applications are trolling motors, and much useful information is available on their performance. The majority of electric boats on the water at this writing use submersible trolling motors. Many trolling motors are used as secondary propulsion units. Most are rated in pounds of thrust and, depending on propeller size, performance varies quite independently of *static thrust* ratings.

TABLE 3-1. DATA ON ELECTRIC OUTBOARDS

Motor Type and Voltage	Current Draw (Amps)	Static Thrust (Pounds)	Electrical Power Consumed* (in Watts)	Thrust Achieved** (Pound-Thrust)	Watts Used Per Pound-Thrust (Watts per Pound)
Submersible 12v	33	27	0.53	0.45	14.7
"	34	20	0.54	0.33	20.4
"	36	33	0.58	0.55	13.1
"	30	20	0.48	0.33	18.0
"	22	12	0.35	0.20	22.0
"	14	8	0.22	0.13	21.0
"	31	21	0.50	0.35	17.7
"	32	21	0.51	0.35	18.3
"	36	24	0.57	0.40	18.0
"	29	15	0.47	0.25	23.5
Submersible 24v	22	22	0.70	0.37	24.0
"	41	40	1.30	0.67	24.6
Above-water 12v	31	28	0.50	0.47	13.3
" " 24v	50	82	1.60	1.37	14.6
" " 36v	65	135	3.12	2.25	17.3
" " 48v	80	195	5.12	3.25	19.7

*(750 watts = 1 horsepower)
**(60 pounds = 1 horsepower)

Static thrust is measured with the motor in a stationary, or static, position where there is no movement of the propulsion system or of the water other than that which passes the propeller. Electric outboards with above-water motors are more powerful than submersibles and are intended for use as a primary power source. Submersible electric motors are more likely to serve as a secondary power source on large boats, but on most electric canoes and similar craft the submersible is the primary source of propulsion. Most submersible units range between 8 and 33 pounds of thrust at a power-use range of 168 to 432 watts, or 0.22 to 0.57 h.p., respectively. Using a mean average, we can assume that 1 h.p. will produce about 60 pounds of static thrust. The *Propeller Handbook* by David Gerr provides us with a formula for approximating static thrust (also called *bollard pull*):

$$T = 62.72 \times (SHP \times D/12)^{0.67}$$

where
T = static thrust in pounds
SHP = shaft horsepower at the propeller
and
D = propeller diameter in inches

Applying the horsepower formula to a relatively common submersible drawing 30 amps at 12 volts, we get 0.48 h.p.

$$(30 \text{ amps} \times 12 \text{ volts})/750 \text{ watts per horsepower} = 0.48 \text{ horsepower}$$

Now we can use the bollard-pull formula to calculate the pounds of static thrust this motor develops turning a 12-inch propeller.

$$T = 62.72 \times (0.48 \times 12/12)^{0.67} = 38 \text{ pounds}$$

To show the nature of actual ratings with a variation in propeller size, consider the same motor with a 6-inch propeller.

$$T = 62.72 \times (0.48 \times 6/12)^{0.67} = 24 \text{ pounds}$$

It is easy to see that the size of the propeller has a significant impact and that static thrust is not necessarily an indicator of overall performance. The static-thrust-to-horsepower ratio *is* a good indicator of efficiency at low speed. Our use of 60 pounds of thrust per horsepower is arbitrary, useful as a comparison guide, and though it may accurately reflect horsepower in some models it will not be accurate for all.

To sum up, we have available 25 amps at 12 volts, or 300 watts. This is equivalent to 0.4 h.p., which will produce about 25 pounds of static thrust for 4 hours, using our standard 12-volt 100-Ah deep-cycle battery, and it gives us an energy density of 20 Wh per pound.

To better put this in perspective, let's consider the fossil-fuel alternative. If we divide rated output by fuel consumption, we find that in a typical modern gasoline-powered generator, 1 fluid ounce of gasoline has the potential to produce about 25 Wh of electricity. So in theory, though not necessarily in practice, the energy stored in our 60-pound battery—1,200 Wh—may be replaced by 48 fluid ounces of gasoline.

$$1,200 \text{ watt-hours}/25 \text{ watt-hours per ounce} = 48 \text{ fluid ounces}$$

The energy density of the gasoline would be 580 Wh per pound.

$$25 \text{ watt-hours per fluid ounce} \times 16 \text{ fluid ounces per pound}$$
$$\times\ 1.45 \text{ ounces per fluid ounce} = 580 \text{ watt-hours per pound}$$

Because gasoline weighs 43 pounds per cubic foot versus water's 62.43, the 1.45 coefficient is required to convert fluid ounces to weight.

From this comparison we see that a pound of gasoline can provide nearly 30 times the energy available from a pound of storage battery. We haven't factored in the oxygen required for combustion that fossil fuel must have to produce energy; taken from the air, oxygen constitutes a large part of the fuel being consumed. The electric storage battery has no such requirement, nor does the storage battery produce any appreciable air pollutants—a claim that cannot be made for the fossil-fuel engine. Of course, unless the electricity stored in our battery came from wind or water power, photovoltaics, or nuclear or exotic fuels, it almost certainly came from burning fossil fuel. Grid power, even from a fossil-fuel grid, is far less polluting (per watt-hour) and more efficient than the portable generator in the above example, an important consideration and one we will examine later in detail.

CATEGORIES OF ELECTRIC WATERCRAFT

It would be difficult, if not impossible, to specify as typical a single craft or a single boating activity for a particular environment, so let's divide watercraft into three categories according to size and usage. This process will also help us to determine what boats are best suited for electric propulsion. For now we are only concerned with energy in the form of electricity derived from a lead-acid battery (or battery bank); i.e., no onboard generator, solar panels, windmills, etc.

Small and Portable

Watercraft in the "small and portable" category can carry from 250 to 600 pounds in live weight and gear. The boat's weight without batteries is between 60 and 130 pounds, making it relatively easy to handle and load. In most cases it will be carried on a car top or truck bed. Its battery bank, usually handled separately, will weigh between 60 and 120 pounds. Our standard 100-Ah battery could be used at the rate of 0.4 h.p. for 4 hours. The speed of a good hull will range from 3 to 6 mph.

What have we gained over the regular canoe or kayak (among which this hull would be grouped) by electrification? We have gained the use of one or both hands at all times while still having excellent control of the craft. We are operating quietly at speeds comparable to boats similar in size and class. We have added stability with the mass of the battery bank. And as we now have an electrical system in place, the operation of other electrical devices such as depth finders, fish finders, or sound systems is an easy option.

ENERGY BASICS AND ELECTRIC PROPULSION

Small electric boats capable of carrying one or two people can be transported on a car top or truck bed. This Black River Guide weighs about 85 pounds and can carry up to 350 pounds.

A "hot" battery and a well-iced cooler make for the beginning of a pleasant day on the water.

What have we sacrificed? Speed is the first thing to come to mind—a 5-h.p. or better gasoline motor can push a planing hull of equivalent weight much faster than our small electric craft, but by virtue of this speed and noise, there is no telling what we might miss. And by now we should be aware of what we'll leave behind for the environment to attempt to digest.

Medium and Trailerable

In the pleasure-boat realm, the trailerable boat is surely the most prevalent. These boats are seen carrying families on weekend outings, delivering anglers to their favorite spots, pulling skiers, or often just occupying space in the carport or garage. Because these boats typically have an extremely high power-to-weight ratio, they are difficult to replace with electric propulsion. For example, the replacement of a 25-h.p. gasoline engine with electrics requires 937 pounds of batteries *for 1 hour of operation.*

$$(25 \text{ horsepower} \times 750 \text{ watts per horsepower} \times 1 \text{ hour})/ \\ 20 \text{ watt-hours per pound} = 937.5 \text{ pounds}$$

Realistically, battery capacity needs to be more like 4,000 pounds for 4 hours of operation, and with this much weight the boat will be unable to achieve planing speed. The only segment of this category of boats that merits consideration for electric propulsion is displacement boats with hull speeds up to about 8 miles per hour. Requiring about 3 h.p., such a boat could operate for 4 hours on a bank of batteries weighing 450 pounds.

$$(3 \text{ horsepower} \times 750 \text{ watts per horsepower} \times 4 \text{ hours})/ \\ 20 \text{ watt-hours per pound} = 450 \text{ pounds}$$

This boat will carry 700 to 1,200 pounds and weigh between 1,000 and 2,000 pounds, battery bank included. Once again we have gained peaceful, quiet operation at relatively low speed with excellent control and stability. We have given up any hopes of pulling a skier or getting back to the scales with that record bass before the other competitors. And our range on the water is significantly restricted.

This handsome Duffield electric boat is easily transported on a trailer and can carry six people on a day's outing. (Photo courtesy Duffield Electric Boats)

Large and In-the-Water

When the boat gets large enough, we are no longer overwhelmed by the weight of our battery bank and may give more consideration to power, range, and comfort. Though most of the boats in the previous categories are recharged away from the water when not in use, the in-the-water boat is docked at its charging station when not underway. As we will see later, this charging station can play a key role in offering power alternatives to the electric grid. For our purpose here, let's choose a generous 10-h.p. and an 8-hour operating cycle—just to set the weight of our battery bank at 3,000 pounds.

$$(10 \text{ horsepower} \times 750 \text{ watts per horsepower} \times 8 \text{ hours})/$$
$$20 \text{ watt-hours per pound} = 3,000 \text{ pounds}$$

Though this is generous and massive, it occupies only 23.5 cubic feet of space that might otherwise contain ballast, centered on the keel under the floor.

$$3,000 \text{ pounds} \times 0.47 \text{ cubic feet}/60 \text{ pounds} = 23.5 \text{ cubic feet}$$

This large mass gives the vessel exceptional stability, and the large electrical reserve provides the opportunity for certain onboard luxuries. An appropriate hull should have a speed of about 7 mph and a range of 50 to 100 miles.

The 30-foot Elco Diana E. Banks, a most traditional electric launch. (Photo courtesy Elco)

Radical Applications

Moving away from our brief overview of the three basic categories, we may learn a bit more about what works best by taking a look at an extreme case. The world

The battery layout of a 30-foot Elco launch. Note also the inboard electric motor. The weight of the batteries and their location add to the stability of the launch. (Photo courtesy Elco)

speed record for an electric boat is a bit over 50 mph. Setting this speed record required just over 2 minutes of operation, but after the record run it took 18 minutes to recharge the battery bank. Even conventional systems presently require almost as much time to replenish the batteries as it takes to discharge them. Though battery weight is certainly a big deficit in some electric boats, the inability to recharge rapidly is the real culprit. A quick way to "fill 'er up," as with a gasoline fuel tank, would bridge a ravenous gap in practicality for electric vehicles of any sort.

MISCONCEPTIONS

The purpose of the above discussion is to provide a realistic look at electrical propulsion. Because electricity cannot be seen or heard, its mysterious qualities lead to some misconceptions that need clearing up.

Batteries

Batteries of the lead–acid variety can be very small and produce, say, 12 volts, or they can be very large and produce only 2 volts. The storage capacity of the battery bank, but not the voltage, is directly related to its mass. Much experimentation is underway with the electrical storage battery, but at this writing all other storage systems are more expensive than lead-acid, and very few are lighter. (We will discuss alternatives to the lead-acid battery in Chapter 6.) The primary objective in much of the experimentation is to improve recharging characteristics. At present, very few alternatives to the lead-acid battery are practical for the rather massive systems of the electric boat.

Solar Power

Using photovoltaics is truly a beautiful way to convert energy from the sun to electricity and should be given the utmost respect. Although the sun provides approximately 1,000 watts per square meter of the earth's surface, the practical energy produced under nearly ideal conditions is only about 400 watts per square meter. Current technology in photovoltaics can convert about 25 percent of this to electrical energy. Therefore, to produce the power needed to propel a small electric boat at about half speed (or one-third power consumption) requires about 100 watts, the output under perfect conditions of a square meter—about 9 square feet—of photovoltaics. Given the usually less than ideal conditions of clouds, poor angle of incidence, smog, shade, and latitude, a more realistic number is 18 square feet, with a battery reserve to assure operation in low- or no-sun conditions. The current cost for this amount of photovoltaics is about $1,350—but photovoltaic (PV) costs continue to decline. Actual insolation, atmospheric conditions, efficiency, and total cost will depend on the area of operation.

The deck or canopy areas of most slender-hulled boats would be hard pressed to carry a collector configuration this large. The roof of a boathouse would provide a better base for an array of PV panels, allowing for greater surface area and for the panels to be properly oriented toward the sun. The installation of photovoltaics on a houseboat, barge, or twin-hull boat could be practical if the expense can be warranted. The energy required to propel a boat at a reasonable speed is usually more than can be produced by sunlight striking the boat's surface area. We should not be disappointed with this limitation, but realize how photovoltaics can best be utilized. Onboard PV panels are ideal for trickle charging, but as a primary power source the panels required would be prohibitively large and are best left to stationary applications. We will note a few exceptions to this when we examine photovoltaics in greater detail in Chapter 8.

Hull Design

Because the energy required to move a boat increases disproportionately with the increase in speed, high speed in electric boats should not be expected. A more important consideration is their clean and quiet operation, and their reliability and simplicity. Given the same amount of energy, it is far more practical to sacrifice speed for extended operating time than it is to sacrifice operating time for higher speed.

The quality of an electric boat is best found in its quiet operation at moderate speed.

With the speed of most electric boats usually well under 10 mph, some hull characteristics are better than others. A good rule of thumb is to look for a hull designed to operate most efficiently at about 3 to 5 mph. As a rule, the longer the waterline the better, keeping in mind the importance of clean lines and minimal wetted surface area. Least applicable to electric propulsion is the planing hull. In the small, medium, and large categories, electric boats are most likely to resemble the canoe or kayak, the displacement launch, and the houseboat, barge, or pontoon boat, respectively.

RANGE

Our overview of electric boats is incomplete without giving some consideration to the tandem concepts of cruising time and speed. We can do this best by focusing not on the type of craft we will be using but on how we intend to spend our time on the water. Agreed, it would be great to have deep reserves of power at our disposal; such reserves could at times be useful. The discipline necessary for conservative use of energy dismisses this, however. This is one characteristic of the electric-boat idea—no unnecessary waste of resources on board or about you. Living with the fixed energy source comfortably leaves you free to concentrate on your purpose on the water. The only two matters that require your attention are time and distance traveled.

A boat that operates most efficiently at 3 to 5 mph would not seem to be a good choice for traversing large bodies of water from point to point. If large distances are to be traveled, much time will be spent on the water. Distance requirements are more applicable to wildlife observation, exploring, or just cruising. While distance may well, at one time or another, become a factor in electric boating, it is the nature of the craft that time on board is of more significance. Going downriver, for example, you can allow the current to carry the boat most of the distance using electric power only for control. This increases time spent on an outing, and range, but a long run might also require either battery replenishment for the trip upstream or a pick-up at the downstream destination. Sometimes great distances can be covered by carefully conserving the use of the electric propulsion.

The time spent on outings may vary, from a lazy afternoon to a demanding cruise of several days. As situations vary, so do the time and power used. For our purpose in looking at the technical aspects of the electric boat, it may be useful to establish a "norm," a target range of operation. Using our standard model of 1,200 watts and 0.4 h.p., we can expect 4 to 6 hours of operation at speeds of 3 to 4 mph, giving us a 9-mile radius, or an 18-mile range. While this may seem small, it is simply an arbitrary benchmark we've used to relay information about motors, batteries, PV systems, controls, etc.

CHAPTER 4

MOTORS AND PROPELLERS

MOTORS

The differences between petroleum-fueled engines and electric motors center on their energy sources. Engines create power by burning the stored energy in fossil fuel directly, while motors produce power by converting electrical energy into mechanical work—just as a dynamo converts mechanical work into electrical energy.

On any vehicle, available electric power is directly limited by the mass of the storage bank. Present storage batteries are massive, their weights limiting the capacity of the vehicle they propel, but it is fortunate that an electric boat can carry more of this mass than most other electric vehicles. Still, this need for storage capacity imposes a limit on the output and type of motor best suited for electric propulsion.

Requirements

Most electric craft are equipped with motors of less than 5 h.p. Keep in mind that for every horsepower used during a 6-hour outing, 225 pounds of battery must be on board.

1 horsepower × 750 watts per horsepower × 6 hours = 4,500 watt-hours
4,500 watt-hours/20 watt-hours per pound = 225 pounds

We have already discussed and ruled out the use of high-horsepower motors—those substantially over 10 h.p.—in electric craft, as they serve only special purposes (e.g., our 50-mph electric boat). Most electric-boat motors will be under 5 h.p. Taking into consideration the prevalence of the electric submersible, or trolling motor, the majority of electric motors used to move watercraft are well under 1 h.p.. The deciding factor in the size of motor required is the size of the craft being propelled. Most craft carrying six passengers or more use 3-h.p. or larger motors to achieve an acceptable speed and range.

The first successful propeller-driven electric boat was also the first outboard motorboat, an 18-foot launch designed and built by Frenchman Gustave Trouve in 1881. Powered by banks of bichromate-potash batteries driving a three-blade propeller, the electric outboard moved the launch up and down the Seine at an average speed of 4.5 mph (Kevin Desmond, *The Guinness Book of Motorboating Facts and Feats*). The electric motor is older than the dynamo, meaning that the earliest electric motors were run from batteries. It was not until generating electricity became practical that the use of the electric motor found its place in industry and later in our homes and everyday affairs. The essential design of electric motors has not changed much in their long existence, although motors may be given different physical characteristics for different purposes.

Of course, AC motors can be quite a bit different from DC motors. The AC or *alternating-current* motor is most often an induction motor utilizing the alternating characteristic of the power; induction motors are rarely used where the power is from a DC source. The DC or *direct-current* motor has two basic forms applicable to electric propulsion, the permanent-magnet motor and the field-wound motor. Motors can be set up for different voltages, which generally depends on the power they are required to produce.

The electric motor produces power when the two essential elements of the motor, the armature and the field, have strong opposing magnetic fields. A magnetic field is produced in the armature by the flow of an electric current, and because the armature is designed to rotate, the "push" of the magnetic field translates the electrical energy into mechanical energy. The field coil of an electric motor functions much like the armature in that in most cases an electric current is used to produce a magnetic field, but the field coil is stationary and in opposition to the field of the armature. Fractional-horsepower motors often use permanent magnets rather than a coil in their fields, simplifying the design and making these motors less expensive to produce. All electric motors are alike in that they translate electrical energy into mechanical energy.

Electrical potentials such as 36 or 48 volts are used for DC motors developing around 2 to 5 h.p., whereas motors in the range of 0.5 h.p. are generally designed for 12- or 24-volt power. Most submersibles produce 0.5 h.p. or less and are almost always 12-volt. An electric motor will operate at less than its stated voltage, but with an accompanying reduction in power output.

The advantage of higher voltage generally relates to greater efficiency as a system's power requirements increase. However, there are other factors to consider before abandoning the 12-volt system. Many small appliances, inverters, motors, batteries, and chargers are designed around the 12-volt system. The small advantage in efficiency in changing from a 12-volt system to a 24-volt system to power a 0.5- h.p. motor may well be offset by the added expense and difficulty in acquiring charging systems and accessories. And two 12-volt batteries are likely to be required since a 24-volt battery is less common and probably more expensive. Most electric craft with 0.5 h.p. or less will be powered by a 12-volt system, and for good reason.

What Size and Type?

Large electric boats are usually equipped with systems using 24- to 48-volt power supplies. These boats are fitted with their own charging and control systems particular to their operating voltages. They frequently have fairly massive battery banks that are kept on board and in place—not removed as with the small 12-volt system. These large banks typically use from two to eight individual batteries, ranging in potential and capacity. Many use the tried and proven 6-volt golf-cart battery—six in series to provide 36 volts, for example—as the power demand and operating time for boats and golf carts are similar.

A significant change in most DC electric motors up to about 3 h.p. is the use of permanent-magnet fields. The magnets used in electric motors are not the old iron magnets—like horseshoe magnets—but rather high-density composites. Most motors using these magnets are rated at less than 0.5 h.p., and permanent-magnet motors are used in all presently manufactured submersibles. The primary advantage of the permanent-magnet motor is the absence of a field wire to draw power or to go bad (usually through corrosion). Disadvantages include the usually small power output and the inability to control speed by controlling the strength of the field. The magnets themselves are also brittle and can be damaged if the unit is subjected to a sudden shock. Because of the prevalence of the submersible, however, the permanent-magnet motor is the most common electric motor in use for watercraft propulsion (see photo on facing page).

Field-wound motors are the norm for most propulsion systems from 2 to 10 h.p., and they necessitate inboard or above-water installation. Field-wound motors differ from permanent-magnet motors in that the field is electrically magnetized. An air cooling system is generally incorporated in the design of field-wound motors—often absent in permanent-magnet motors. Useful efficiency comparisons between low-power and high-power electric boat motors are complicated by the fact that the smaller motors are almost always permanent-magnet while the larger motors are field-wound.

A 24-volt permanent-magnet motor for use inboard. This motor has a 0.5-h.p. output at 1,125 rpm. (Photo courtesy Budsin Woodcraft)

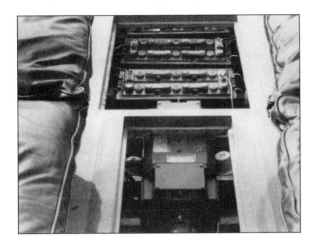

A 48-volt field-wound motor rated 5 h.p. at 1,100 rpm. (Photo courtesy Elco)

One of the distinct differences between the two motors is in the relationship between electrical polarity and each motor's direction of rotation. When polarity is reversed, the direction of rotation of a permanent-magnet motor is also reversed. This is not the case for the field-wound motor because the polarity reversal reverses the current in both the field coil and the armature, so the motor continues to run in the direction for which it was set up. In order to reverse the rotation, the polarity of either the armature or of the field *only* must be reversed. This is of little real significance except that it needs to be taken into account when choosing a control system. The field-wound direct-current motor is one of the oldest types of motors and remains the best choice for units requiring 3 or more horsepower. The usual shaft speed of permanent-magnet submersibles using a direct drive is about 1,100 revolutions per minute (rpm). The speeds of field-wound motors and inboard permanent-magnet motors typically range from 1,100 to 3,100 rpm. Lower propeller speeds are usually necessary for motors turning 1,600 rpm or better and are achieved through the use of some kind of reduction gear.

Maintenance

There is little to go wrong with an electric motor, especially in electric-boat applications. Submersible motors run scant risk of overheating except in the event of a locked or restricted propeller, and in this instance a simple electrical fuse system will provide adequate protection from damage. The corrosive action of salt water is, of course, just as detrimental to electric motors as it is to gasoline engines, and measures should be taken to protect the motor from this environment. Accidental flooding with fresh water is not particularly good, but it rarely has a lasting detrimental effect if discovered early and the motor is cleaned and dried out as soon as possible. Resistance windings in some submersibles sometimes become damaged and adversely affect the step speed control designed into these motors.

The fact is, a properly cared-for electric motor will almost never wear out. Cleaning and occasional brush replacement seem to be all that is normally necessary to keep such motors running as good as new. In all my many outings, I've never been let down by an electric motor. Once I inadvertently left a flooded submersible motor filled with water for a long period. When I discovered it, cleaning the unit and replacing the seals were all that was required to renew the motor. This problem can be avoided by allowing the motor to drain between uses, especially if you think the motor might have been flooded. During operation, small amounts of water evaporate from a submersible motor through the motor tube, which should never be closed off.

Cost of Operation

Electricity purchased from the utility company generally costs no more than about 10 cents per kilowatt-hour (1kWh = 1,000 Wh). If a recharging system is only 75 percent efficient, taking into account heat losses in both the battery and charger, we can replenish our standard battery from the grid for about 16 cents.

$$1,200 \text{ watt-hours}/0.75 = 1,600 \text{ watt-hours}$$
$$1,600 \text{ watt-hours} \times \$0.10 \text{ per kilowatt-hour} = \$0.16$$

We saw in Chapter 3 that producing this same 1,200 Wh from a small fossil-fuel-powered generator requires about 48 fluid ounces of fuel. Pegging the price of gasoline at an even \$1.00 per gallon and taking the same heat losses into account, it costs about 50 cents to recharge our battery with the small generator.

$$48 \text{ fluid ounces}/0.75 \times \$1.00/128 \text{ fluid ounces} = \$0.50$$

The above calculations show two things clearly. One is that electric boats use their energy very conservatively. Operating a 5-h.p. vessel at full speed for 4 hours costs only \$2.00 if the power is replenished from the grid.

$$750 \text{ watts per horsepower} \times 5 \text{ horsepower} \times 4 \text{ hours} = 15{,}000 \text{ watt-hours}$$
$$15{,}000 \text{ watt-hours}/0.75 \times \$0.10 \text{ per kilowatt-hour} = \$2.00$$

The second point is that the electric company is more efficient at producing power than is the smaller fossil-fuel generator. We should also take into account that power from the grid might not all be generated from burning fossil fuel. Never to be forgotten is that the sun provides us with free energy. If the investment to convert this energy to its electrical form can be warranted, photovoltaics, wind, and water power can provide the cleanest nonpolluting forms of energy. More will be said about charging in Chapter 7.

The electric motor and the lead-acid battery have both been around for a long time, and opportunities to put them to good use have been around equally as long. Now is the time to put them to good use in a quiet and conservative electric boat.

PROPELLERS

The propeller, or in nautical jargon, the *wheel*, is, like the automobile wheel, the component that transfers power. The propeller is the driving force that pushes, pulls, squirts, or cuts the water to produce movement. Given enough power, it can produce high speeds or push great masses. It has many configurations, comes in many sizes, and in many ways is the most complex component of a powerboat, regardless whether fossil fuel or electricity powers it.

The limited energy source of an electric boat necessitates an efficient propeller, and the inherently quiet nature of electric power suggests a quiet propeller as well. It may operate near the surface in a vessel with shallow draft, or it may be installed deeper in the case where water depth is of less concern. Few

A 9-inch x 4-inch three-blade bronze propeller. (Photo courtesy Budsin Woodcraft)

other components of a boat require dealing with as many variables as choosing the right wheel. In the case of the electric boat, high speed—above 10 mph—is one factor that can be dropped immediately. We are left to choose the correct propeller to convert 0.5 to 10 h.p. into boat velocity as quietly and efficiently as possible.

There are three basic factors affecting propeller performance and efficiency: diameter, speed in revolutions per minute (rpm), and pitch.

Propeller Diameter

Diameter is the most critical factor in determining the amount of power a propeller absorbs and transmits. The thrust necessary to move a boat at displacement speeds has a direct relationship to the diameter of the prop. Recalling the formula from Chapter 3 for calculating static thrust, or bollard pull, we can use it to calculate the effect of a change in the diameter of the propeller, all other factors remaining the same.

$$T = 62.72 \times (SHP \times D/12)^{0.67}$$

Pegging our shaft horsepower (SHP) at the propeller at 1, we can solve the formula for propellers 6 inches and 12 inches in diameter:

$$T = 62.72 \times (1 \times 6/12)^{0.67} = 39.5 \text{ pounds}$$
$$T = 62.72 \times (1 \times 12/12)^{0.67} = 62.7 \text{ pounds}$$

The formula assumes ideal conditions; displacement hulls in the range we are concerned with for electric boats that use large propellers at slow shaft speeds may achieve a static thrust approaching 90 percent of the formula value. Static thrust is not the prerequisite for selecting propeller diameter, but it is an indicator of performance and efficiency. In *The Propeller Handbook* Dave Gerr tells us that the ideal theoretical size for a propeller is one-third the beam of the vessel, but in practical applications a propeller this large might not always be possible. Practical limits are determined by draft, hull design, and shaft rpm. The maximum diameter of the propeller for a deep-water electric pleasure boat, for example, is likely to be limited by the effective shaft rpm, while the determining limitation for an electric canoe is more likely to be its shallow draft.

Turning again to Gerr's *Propeller Handbook*, we find a formula we can use to calculate the *minimum effective propeller diameter in inches* (D_{min}) for a given application. This, in combination with the ideal propeller diameter, will establish a range within which our selected propeller should fall.

$$D_{min} = 4.07 \times \sqrt{(BWL \times Hd)}$$
where
BWL = beam on the waterline in feet
and
Hd = draft of the hull in feet (excluding skeg)

A waterline beam of 4 feet and a draft of 12 inches would be rather typical for an electric boat about 16 feet long.

$$D_{min} = 4.07 \times \sqrt{(4 \times 1)} = 8 \text{ inches}$$

Our ideal theoretical propeller is:

$$D_{max} = 1/3 \times 4 \text{ feet} \times 12 \text{ inches per foot} = 16 \text{ inches}$$

If you choose to use a larger propeller without regard to draft, it will be necessary to determine the pitch and the shaft speed.

Shaft RPM

On the proven premise that the larger and slower turning the propeller the better, we will consider the shaft speed. Here we must look for a compromise between the motor's most effective operating speed and the most efficient shaft speed. We have already established that electric motors commonly used for boat propulsion typically operate within a speed range from 1,100 to 3,100 rpm to produce their peak power. Direct drive for smaller propellers is most often used for motors turning at about 1,100 rpm. Turning a large propeller at an efficient speed usually requires a reduction of 3:1 to 10:1 in motor to shaft speed. The loss in efficiency through reduction is easily offset by the increased efficiency of the larger propeller as well as its quieter operation.

The extraordinarily helpful *Propeller Handbook* also gives us a formula for calculating the most efficient shaft speed for a particular propeller installation. Assuming a shaft horsepower (SHP) of 3, we can determine the ideal shaft speed for the 16-foot electric boat in our example:

$$rpm^{0.6} = (632.7 \times SHP^{0.2})/D$$
$$rpm^{0.6} = (632.7 \times 1.245)/16 = 49.23$$
$$rpm = 661.28, \text{ or about } 700 \text{ rpm}$$

To turn the propeller at this speed requires a 3:1 reduction for a 2,100-rpm motor.

Pitch

For our spinning propeller to move the boat forward, the propeller must have some degree of pitch. The pitch of the blades is often equated to the threads of a screw (which is why the prop is often referred to as the *screw*). *Pitch* is the measurement of how far forward a propeller would travel during one revolution if it were cutting its way through a solid mass. For example, the theoretical advance of a propeller with a 12-inch pitch would be 12 inches per revolution. But water isn't a solid, so the actual advance of the propeller is always less than the theoretical calculation. This difference is termed *slip*. The degree of slip depends largely on the speed of the boat and its hull configuration. A planing boat with a speed of 70 mph may experience prop slip of around 10 percent, whereas a boat with a hull configuration and in the

*The product of pitch
times rpm gives the
theoretical propeller
advance. Actual
forward travel of the
boat is reduced by the
prop slip.*

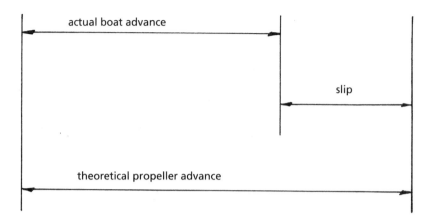

size range of our electric craft, operating at speeds of less than 10 mph, is likely to experience prop slip closer to 45 percent. Slip and efficiency are not the same.

Propellers are designated by diameter and pitch. For example, a 12-inch diameter propeller with a theoretical advance of 12 inches per revolution would be specified as a 12 × 12 propeller—sometimes referred to as a "square" wheel. (The first number is always diameter.) There's nothing special about the diameter and the pitch being the same other than that in many applications it works out that way. The relationship between pitch and diameter is referred to as the *pitch ratio*, which is the pitch in inches divided by the diameter in inches. From Gerr's *Propeller Handbook*, we find that the pitch ratio for craft operating at 8 mph is about 0.8. For a 12-inch diameter propeller, this ratio yields a pitch of 10 inches; i.e., a 12 × 10 propeller.

If we consider using the ideal 16-inch propeller turning at the ideal 700 rpm to push our 3-h.p., 16-foot electric boat, can we also determine the ideal pitch? The answer is yes, and without a great deal of complexity.

At 6 mph, we are moving at 528 feet per minute.

$$(6 \text{ miles per hour} \times 1 \text{ hour}/60 \text{ minutes}) \times (5{,}280 \text{ feet}/1 \text{ mile}) = 528 \text{ feet per minute}$$

From our big, slow-turning prop we expect prop slip to be about 45 percent, so we need to allow for this lost forward motion. Given this degree of slip, our 528 feet of forward motion is only 55 percent of the theoretical forward movement of the propeller, which we can easily calculate to be 960 feet.

$$528 \text{ feet}/0.55 = 960 \text{ feet}$$

In other words, our propeller must advance at the rate of 960 feet per minute to achieve a boatspeed of 528 feet per minute, or 6 mph. Therefore the pitch (P) of this propeller will be 16.5 inches.

$$P = (960 \text{ feet per minute}/700 \text{ rpm}) \times 12 \text{ inches per foot} =$$
$$16.5 \text{ inches per revolution}$$

Our propeller in this case would probably be designated as 16 × 16, which just happens to be a square wheel.

You should have noticed that the above pitch calculation is independent of the diameter of the propeller. So if we fit our boat with a propeller of the minimum diameter—8 inches in this case—the pitch would still need to be 16 inches or better to achieve 6 mph at 700 rpm. This gives us a pitch ratio of 2—not a good choice. The greater the pitch, the more energy the blade uses pushing water aside rather than astern. By doubling the shaft speed to 1,400 rpm we reduce the calculated pitch by half—to 8 inches.

$$P = (960 \text{ feet per minute}/1,400 \text{ rpm}) \times 12 \text{ inches per foot} =$$
$$8.2 \text{ inches per revolution}$$

This 8 × 8 propeller is more effective at higher speeds than we expect from an electric boat, but it could be useful on boats with direct drive and/or shallow draft.

Blade Configuration

Ideally a boat propeller should have a single blade so that this one blade is always working in undisturbed water, but this isn't practical since a single blade can't be balanced. Two opposing blades would seem to be the logical solution, and this configuration is practical for high-speed vessels, but in low-speed applications it necessitates a large-diameter prop to get the surface area needed. The three-blade propeller, the most common design, seems to provide the best compromise between balance, blade area, and efficiency. The use of more than three blades could allow for a reduction in propeller diameter though the resulting prop might not be as efficient.

Summary

For powerboats in general, numerous factors must be considered for propeller selection, but the majority of these are related to high-speed operation or highly loaded blades, which we need not consider for electric boats. Admittedly, the expected performance of a propeller intended for a craft cruising at speeds of 6 mph cannot be based on the prop's bollard pull alone, but there are some valid generalizations about low-speed displacement-boat propellers that fall into a category of reasonable expectations: larger is better, slower is quieter, and proper pitch for the power rating of an electric motor usually requires a reduction to lower shaft speed.

The slip factor of a propeller is determined to a large extent by the hull configuration, and there's no better way to improve speed and efficiency than through the design of the hull. Motors can be loaded to their rated power by the pitch of the propeller, and appropriate pitch selection will vary depending upon the expected speed of the boat.

In small boats such as the electric canoe, where propeller diameter must be small because of draft or direct drive of the submersible unit, speed and a degree of quiet operation are sometimes sacrificed. Many of the stock props for electric outboards, however, are designed to push heavy loads at low speeds—under 4 mph. With a long, lean hull, small boats can move faster than the design speed of most of the standard propellers supplied with electric trolling motors. The increased efficiency of multiple blades should be considered, as should increased pitch—provided it doesn't overload the motor at hull speed.

CHAPTER 5

ELECTRICAL CONTROLS

TWO ATTRACTIVE CHARACTERISTICS of the electric boat are quiet operation and precise control. Inherent in the boat's electric motor is the ability to provide smooth and quiet power from a stored electricity source. The characteristics of direct-current electric motors and storage batteries combine to dictate the requirements for varying the level of power output, a not-always-simple proposition. The power produced by an internal-combustion engine is rather simply controlled by limiting its fuel-air intake, but the "fuel" for an electric motor is supplied from a fixed power source. Our standard battery, for example, is ready to provide 100 amps at 12 volts DC immediately upon tapping. To vary the output of our electric motor, we must be able to manipulate this power source through some type of control device. Allowing the motor to draw all of its designed potential would mean full-speed operation continuously until the motor was disconnected from the power source or until the power source was depleted.

Historically, several methods of speed control have been used in the power link between the electric motor and the battery source. At present, most motors up to 5 h.p. use a pulse-width modulating (PWM) device, but other methods of power control still have merit and in some cases demonstrate advantages over this solid-state system. In the following paragraphs we will look at the points of merit as well as the disadvantages of some commonly used control systems.

The output power delivered by an electric motor is most directly controlled by the amount of electrical power provided to it. We already know from our formula for calculating electrical power ($P = V \times A$) that a reduction in the voltage of our power source produces a corresponding reduction in the level of electrical power supplied, and this results in a similar reduction in the output power of our motor. This reduction of the voltage to the motor is most obviously accomplished by lowering the source voltage. For example, with a 12-volt battery bank composed of two 6-volt batteries, we could use only one battery to provide only 6 volts to our motor. This is referred to as *battery switching* or *tapping.* In large systems using many 6-volt batteries to make up, say, a 48-volt battery bank, it is possible to provide eight stepped power settings in 6-volt increments.

From the above formula we can see that a reduction in current (amperage) will also produce a reduction in the level of electrical power. Smaller electrical systems, such as our 12-volt canoe, use this principle to achieve power control, employing resistors to limit the flow of electrical current to the motor. This is the simplest of the power-control systems, and we will start with it in its various configurations.

METHODS OF POWER CONTROL

Power Control Using Electrical Resistance

Electrical resistance is opposition to the flow of electricity. Resistance is independent of the direction of the current, and it results in the production of heat. The relationship among current, potential, and resistance is expressed by a simple formula known as Ohm's Law. This law states that the current (I) through a conductor is directly proportional to the potential difference (V) between the ends of the conductor and inversely proportional to the resistance (R) of the conductor. Stated more concisely, I is proportional to V/R, which gives us the formula for Ohm's Law:

$$I = V/R$$

The unit of resistance is the *ohm,* so designated in honor of the 19th-century German high-school teacher George Ohm. His enunciation of this law in 1827 aroused such bitter antagonism that he lost his position. Years later, when his work was corroborated by other scientists, he was honored by a professorship in physics at the University of Munich, according to a delightful old physics book my Uncle Luther used in college that presented simple things in a simple manner.

We can rearrange this formula as:

$$V = IR$$

Plugging the units of measurement—the volt, the ampere, and the ohm—into the formula, we find that

$$1 \text{ volt} = 1 \text{ ampere} \times 1 \text{ ohm}$$

With Ohm's Law behind us, let's press on, beginning with a two-speed system using a single resistor. Our sample 300-watt motor uses 25 amps at 12 volts to produce its maximum power output. To reduce the motor's power output by 50 percent, we must limit the input power to 150 watts by adding resistance in series with the motor.

A simple two-speed resistance controller.

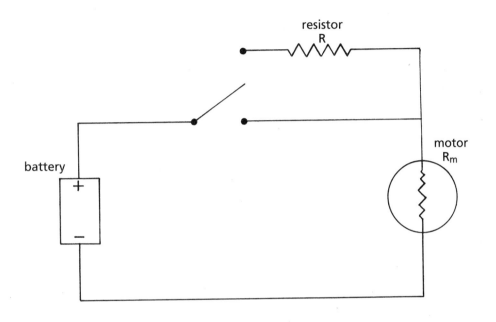

To determine the right amount of resistance, we need to know the internal resistance (R_m) of our motor. We can determine this using Ohm's law, stated a third way:

$$R = V/I$$
$$R_m = 12 \text{ volts}/25 \text{ amps} = 0.48 \text{ ohms}$$

Now we want to increase the resistance of the circuit to reduce the power available to the motor to 150 watts. Total power is equal to the sum of the power consumed by the individual components—in this case the motor and the resistor:

$$P \text{ total} = P \text{ motor} + P \text{ resistor}$$

ELECTRICAL CONTROLS

From Chapter 3 we know that P = VA, which we can also state as P = VI (A and I both representing current in amps). Using V = IR and P = VI, we can derive by substitution:

$$P = I^2R$$

Knowing the power needed at the motor—150 watts—and its internal resistance—0.48 ohms—we can determine the current in the circuit.

$$P_m = I^2R_m$$

or

$$I = \sqrt{(P_m/R_m)}$$
$$I = \sqrt{(150 \text{ watts}/0.48 \text{ ohms})} = 17.68 \text{ amps}$$

Now, knowing that we are dealing with a 12-volt source, we can calculate the total power used in this system and how it is used.

$$P \text{ total} = 12 \text{ volts} \times 17.68 \text{ amps} = 212 \text{ watts}$$
$$P \text{ resistor} = 212 \text{ watts} - 150 \text{ watts} = 62 \text{ watts}$$
$$R \text{ resistor} = 62 \text{ watts}/(17.68 \text{ amps})^2 = 0.2 \text{ ohms}$$

The value of our resistor would be 0.2 ohms.

To reduce the power to the motor to 150 watts, we have had to waste in resistance heating some 62 watts, or 29 percent of the total power consumed by the system. This power wastage is the largest fault in resistance speed control for fixed or limited stored sources. Nonetheless, it is still a simple and effective method.

Many submersibles use fixed resistance in one or more resistors to provide an incremental speed control in as few as two to as many as twelve steps. The resistors are mounted in the motor housing where they are cooled by the surrounding water—and subject to destruction by corrosion if the motor becomes flooded and is not cleaned promptly. If this occurs, one or more of the steps may be lost, but maximum power will be unaffected. Such disabled motors are prime candidates for adapting to a variable speed control through a variable rheostat or a phase-width modulating system.

The Rheostat

The rheostat is also a resistance method of limiting power to the motor. It differs in that the resistance is not incremental but variable; a rheostat is literally a variable resistor. Using a rheostat is an easy and inexpensive way to achieve variable speed control for small motors.

To calculate the size and capacity of the rheostat required we will again use our

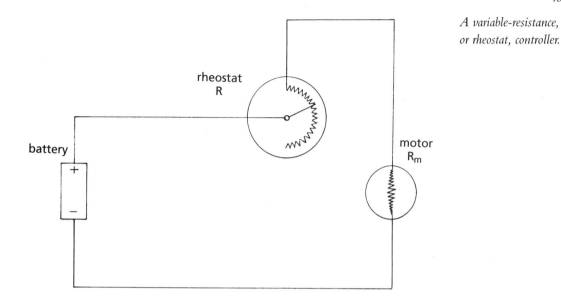

sample motor. We need only be certain that the resistor's capacity in watts is the same as or greater than the wattage of the motor. Because it will be operating in its higher resistance range most of the time, the lower portion of the rheostat will usually see little use. For our sample motor, we select a rheostat with a 300-watt capacity. Next we need to determine its resistance value. Let's assume we want our lowest input to be 2 percent, or 6 watts.

$$I = \sqrt{(P/R)}$$
$$I = \sqrt{(6 \text{ watts}/0.48 \text{ ohms})} = 3.5 \text{ amps}$$
$$P \text{ total} = 12 \text{ volts} \times 3.5 \text{ amps} = 42 \text{ watts}$$
$$P \text{ resistor} = 42 \text{ watts} - 6 \text{ watts} = 36 \text{ watts}$$
$$R \text{ resistor} = 36 \text{ watts}/(3.5 \text{ amps})^2 = 2.9 \text{ ohms}$$

The resistance value of our rheostat should be about 3 ohms.

With this control system, more than 80 percent of the energy used in the low-speed operation of our motor is lost as waste heat. We have exact speed control, but at a cost of 36 watts of power while using 6 watts at the propeller. The

1,200-Wh source may not notice this much lost power until it comes time to head back to the hill. You could end up paddling to pay for your losses.

Battery Switching

Battery switching is another method of speed control. This system is often seen aboard larger craft that use many individual batteries to make up their banks, but it isn't common in small systems. In some respects, switching is the most efficient method of speed control, but it isn't without shortcomings. The uneven discharging of the battery bank places more stress on some of the batteries in the bank and less on others, and the uneven discharge creates additional problems in the recharging process (which we discuss in Chapter 7). Also, the switches involved are complex and they must not fail or a serious short could result. And even though this may be the most efficient method of providing only the power needed—without any loss to resistors—it still has the disadvantage of providing stepped or incremental power.

A four-step speed control using battery switching.

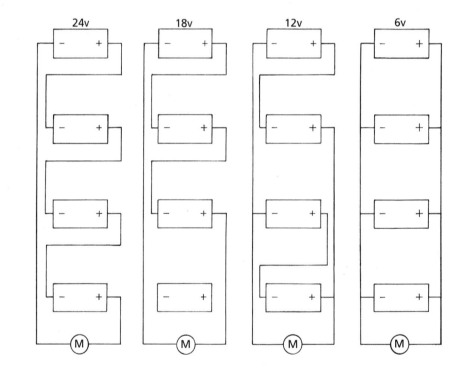

Using a battery bank with a 24-volt potential made up of four individual 6-volt batteries, we could devise a control system that could supply 6, 12, 18, or 24 volts to our motor, giving us four incremental speeds. First, we need to know the internal resistance of our sample 300-watt motor, set up this time for 24-volt operation.

$$I = 300 \text{ watts}/24 \text{ volts} = 12.5 \text{ amps}$$
$$R = 24 \text{ volts}/12.5 \text{ amps} = 1.9 \text{ ohms}$$

Now we make our power calculations for the four supply voltage levels.

$$I = 6 \text{ volts}/1.9 \text{ ohms} = 3.1 \text{ amps}$$
$$P = 6 \text{ volts} \times 3.1 \text{ amps} = 18.6 \text{ watts}$$

$$I = 12 \text{ volts}/1.9 \text{ ohms} = 6.3 \text{ amps}$$
$$P = 12 \text{ volts} \times 6.3 \text{ amps} = 75.6 \text{ watts}$$

$$I = 18 \text{ volts}/1.9 \text{ ohms} = 9.5 \text{ amps}$$
$$P = 18 \text{ volts} \times 9.5 \text{ amps} = 171 \text{ watts}$$

$$P = 24 \text{ volts} \times 12.5 \text{ amps} = 300 \text{ watts}$$

These four different supply voltages give us the choice of four speeds at 6.2, 25.2, 57, and 100 percent of full power. Our 6.2-percent configuration requires all the 6-volt batteries to be wired in parallel. The next step requires the parallel connection of *pairs* of batteries wired in series. Our 18-volt setup has three batteries wired in series with the fourth one left out (or connected in parallel with one of the others). Operating the system at this voltage results in uneven depletion of the battery bank. The final step—full power—is the connection of all four batteries in series to provide 24 volts.

With battery switching, no energy is lost to a resistance placed in-line for control purposes; control is provided through a complex array of contacts or relays. But these switches are required to handle high amperages, and any failure could have dramatic results. Switches capable of handling this demand have become almost prohibitively expensive.

Pulse-Width Modulation

Most electric motors currently being installed for primary propulsion applications, regardless of type or installation, rely on PWM speed control systems. This solid-state system has many advantages over both resistor and battery-switching methods of speed control, the first and foremost being its nonincremental or infinitely variable operating characteristic. The variable resistors used on small trolling motors to limit the output power, allowing small fishing boats to hold fixed positions by matching boatspeed to current speed, are giving way to PWM systems.

The advantages of variable speed control are easily overlooked unless experienced firsthand. Other than matching current speed, it also allows you to match the speed of accompanying boats during encounters or when traveling in groups. Traveling rail to rail for conversation or passing items from one craft to another is a luxury not afforded by a step system. Perhaps most important is the ability of the variable speed control to select the most efficient speed for the load and conditions under which the craft is operating. This device in combination with proper instruments can make energy planning much more effective and in turn give greater peace of mind to the operator.

Elco motor control rated at 5 h.p., 48 volts DC, 100 amps DC. This control allows forward and reverse operation at variable speeds. (Photo courtesy Elco)

PWM systems are not 100 percent efficient, but they are far more efficient than resistor systems and safer and easier on battery banks than battery switching. Excluding some of the smaller, inexpensive outboards, PWM systems have in effect become the standard power control for electric watercraft. Most operate at 90-percent efficiency or better, a small loss compared with the alternatives. For full-throttle operation to deliver all potential power to the motor, a simple bypass switch is practical for some units to provide maximum efficiency at maximum output. The bypass switch cuts out the PWM system, providing more power for strong currents or when speed takes precedence over economy. It also avoids subjecting the controller to full-load operation.

The nature of PWM systems allows the control throttle to be as small as a 1-inch cube at the end of a length of cable or to be operated with a wireless remote control. The main body of the system may be as small as a cigarette pack or as large as a breadbox. Some of the components require cooling—sometimes with small fans, sometimes with water, but most often through finned heat sinks.

Although the engineering of PWM systems is well beyond the scope of this book, how they work is easy enough to understand. The term "pulse-width modulation" comes from the principal operating characteristic of the device. It can best be pictured as an electric gate with a very fast open/close switch. The gate contains the power source. On one side of the gate is all the power of the battery and on the other side is the waiting motor. The gate is either open or closed, and its state at any time is controlled by the switch. Through this gate all the power—except for the minute amount drawn by the switch—flows to the motor. Inherent in the gate, as in the resistor, is some loss of power to heat, which means that it requires cooling. If the gate and switch are integral, cooling is accomplished using heat sinks or air fans, but if the two components are kept separate, the gate can be water-cooled, either in the hull or, in the case of the outboard submersible, in the motor tube. The gate handles the muscle whereas the switch serves as the brains.

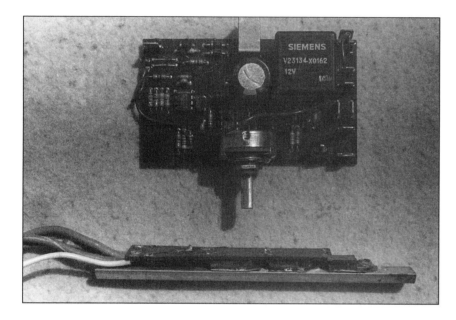

The main components of a PWM speed controller rated at 30 amps at 12 volts DC made for use with a submersible motor. Top: *the switch with integral potentiometer.* Bottom: *the gate, mounted to its heat sink.*

The switch provides simple open-close signals to the gate. It does this very rapidly and usually at a frequency above the audible range, although early units—and even some present PWM systems where noise is not a factor—operate at the top of the audible range. This produces a high-pitched squeal that, while not loud, can be quite irritating. The duration of each On pulse—*the pulse width*—determines the average total energy allowed through the gate; the greater the duration of the open signal, the greater the power being transferred from the battery bank to the motor. This pulse width is usually controlled by a small *potentiometer* (a variable resistor) that can be mounted quite easily in locations remote from both the switch and gate, using very light leads. This makes PWM control especially suitable for small craft, where space and aesthetics are at a premium and the degree of control afforded by having all controls in the tiller handle is much sought after.

Of the three methods of motor-speed control, the PWM system, with its infinitely variable range, high efficiency, and component design, is the most attractive and practical. Do not rule out other methods, such as the rheostat, when cost or availability is a factor. In some applications, efficiency may take a back seat to economy.

Motor Rotation Reversal

Reverse, even if used infrequently, is still all but essential in most boats. With electric power, reversing the direction of motor rotation is usually accomplished simply by reversing the polarity. In the case of a resistance control system, reversing the polarity at either the battery or the motor is permissible. The same applies to battery switching. The PWM system, however, restricts reversing to the motor only, as the polarity of the system itself cannot be reversed. This usually presents few problems as long as the reversing switch is installed in the motor leads. With a PWM system, it is often best to use a *relay switch* for reversing, which allows a smaller control switch to be installed conveniently in the instrument panel or the tiller handle. Remember that field-wound motors must be reversed by reversing either the field or armature leads only.

INSTRUMENTS AND GAUGES

Power usage has greater significance for the electric boat than for craft powered by fossil fuel. On the electric boat we are unable to shake the fuel tank or visually determine what fuel is on board; the battery looks and weighs the same whether full or empty, and we must rely on instruments to measure what is available. Knowing the state of the battery's charge is the single most important piece of information to have. The assumption that the charger has done its job is only that, unless verified.

The first electric boat motor I ever owned was a Phantom Bantam, which I used many years ago as an auxiliary for sailing on a nearby lake. I ran it from a battery that was kept up at the local gas station and had always performed admirably. I always assumed it was fully charged when I went to the lake. My wife-to-be and I went sailing one hot July day. The wind started out well and we moved far from port, enjoying our outing. That afternoon the wind went dead, and much to my dismay, so was the battery. The water was so calm you could see a bug hit it a quarter-mile away. That event contributed to the sale of that little motor, which was never at fault.

Since that time, I have often kept the battery for a small boat in my truck's battery box. Besides providing a more-or-less free recharge, the truck has an accurate *ammeter* that shows me when the battery is up and no longer accepting a charge. This is my guarantee that the past will not repeat itself.

When the batteries are removed for charging, we can determine the state of charge by testing the fluid in the cells with a *hydrometer*—available for a few dollars at any autoparts store. When the battery bank is a permanent installation, usually well concealed, inspection of individual batteries and cells is not so easy. In either case, a *voltmeter* can determine the state of charge with less effort.

The Voltmeter

An accurate voltage reading is one way to determine a battery's state of charge, and it is the only way to check a sealed battery. However, the open-circuit voltage of a battery or bank of batteries varies little from fully charged to discharged. In the case of the 12-volt battery, this range is from 12.2 to 12.8 volts. Voltage readings are most accurate when the battery has been at rest for some minutes, and they aren't valid for determining the level of charge when the batteries are under a load or in use. Even then, useful information can be gathered from the voltmeter once the operator is familiar with the battery bank and the operation of his or her craft. Meters showing the state of charge as an ordinary fuel reading are simple to read, but an expanded-scale voltmeter—one reading only the range of voltages you are concerned with (see photo)—is more useful. State-of-charge estimates based on voltmeter readings will also be more accurate for higher-voltage battery banks (36- or 48-volt, for instance) because the higher potential expands the narrow area from charge to discharge.

A DC voltmeter available at most autoparts or discount stores. Unless charging on board, only the range between 11 and 13 volts is used.

The Ammeter

The ammeter is the most accurate way to monitor power usage. Its range should be selected in accordance with the normal current draw. For example, a motor that draws 25 amps could use a 30-amp gauge; a gauge with a 100-amp range would be relatively insensitive and more difficult to read accurately.

For a boat with an onboard charging system, an ammeter capable of measuring the flow of current in both directions—charge and discharge—is an excellent choice. This will enable the operator to determine the battery's acceptance of charge or state of discharge and also provide a means of monitoring power consumption

To measure current consumption, an ammeter needs to read in only one direction; this one measures current flow in both directions and is appropriate for craft with onboard charging systems.

when operating from reserves.

With an ammeter and knowledge of your battery bank's rating and capacity, you can accurately calculate your range and speed. For example, our standard 12-volt 100-Ah battery is rated at 5 amps for 20 hours, so we can assume that with a draw of 5 amps—as registered on the gauge—we can operate our craft for 20 hours. Actual experience with an individual system can lead to very accurate calculations of range and speed—assuming you have also accurately assessed the battery's state of charge and you aren't unwittingly starting out with less than a "full tank."

SWITCHES AND RELAYS

Electric motors big enough to propel a boat draw a lot of amps. Undersized wires, switches, or relays cause a loss in efficiency and perhaps even total failure. For this reason, the larger the motor, the higher the voltage at which it should be operated. Consider a 1-h.p. motor operating at 12 volts. The full-power current draw in this case would be 62.5 amps.

$$P = VI \text{ or } I = P/V$$
$$I = (1 \text{ horsepower} \times 750 \text{ watts per horsepower})/12 \text{ volts}$$
$$I = 62.5 \text{ amps}$$

This is a substantial amount of current, requiring huge wire leads and switches. (For more on wire sizes, see Appendix B.) But the same motor operating at 36 volts draws only one-third of this amount, or 20.8 amps—well within the capacity of reasonably priced wires and switches.

Because storage batteries have large amounts of power available immediately on demand, precautions against shorting and arcing should always be in mind. Protection through fusing is required in all but the simplest systems; few things are more unpleasant or dangerous than a battery releasing its total bank of energy into a set of melting, burning wires. Select a fuse value that will prevent a meltdown, but not such a low rating that the fuse blows out every time the motor happens to become momentarily overloaded. A good rule of thumb is to install a fuse equal to 125 percent of total amperage. Always install fuses in the *hot* lead, never in the ground wire.

Every electric boat with reverse has a double-pole switch or relay somewhere in the line. In the case of permanent-magnet motors, this particular switch carries a load at all times, so power losses in this switch affect both forward and reverse operation. Other than the power control, this is the most important switch in the system. In many applications this switch can only be operated after bringing the motor to a full stop. This prevents the accidental—or intentional—loading of the system caused by switching polarity at speed, which is not good practice. I find myself all too often popping reverse to clear a leaf-fouled prop—unnecessary, but in a tight spot I do it. I prefer to have this capability, but I also recognize the cost in switches and damage potential.

SUMMARY

Considering the simplicity of the DC electric motor, especially the permanent-magnet type, speed and direction (reversing) controls are the most complex electrical components of the electric boat. Consequently, they are often the most expensive and the most difficult to be made absolutely reliable. It will serve the electric-boat operator to know the control system well—how to repair or replace it and how to bypass it in the event of an emergency. The simplest method of providing a backup in the event of a PWM breakdown is to install a bypass switch, a useful feature in any case to remove the PWM controller from the system at top speed. This allows all the available power to be delivered to the motor and avoids subjecting the controller to full-load operation.

Battery switching has its points but is rarely used today, partly because the cost of the required mechanical contacts has become prohibitive. Resistance step-speed is reliable and is usually a built-in feature of small submersible motors. Use it if it's there, and try not to envy too much the smooth performance of the boat at your rail using

The instrument panel of a 16-foot electric canoe showing volt and amp meters and controller bypass, on-off, and forward-reverse switches. The speed-control tuner is mounted in the tiller handle (not shown).

PWM. The use of variable resistors will die hard because they are cheap and effective, and the anglers using them are more interested in fishing than power consumption.

A good speed control, like the accelerator of an automobile, allows the operator to control his or her craft in a precise manner. And good instruments can help to make a good captain out of most of us, raising the degree of confidence in the ability of our vessel and in our control to that of the power-station manager. Instruments also allow for and encourage the planning so important in the use of a fixed energy source.

CHAPTER 6

BATTERIES

THERE IS LITTLE DOUBT that the limited capacity to store electrical energy is the single greatest shortcoming of every electric vehicle, including the electric boat. Methods of generating onboard electrical energy without using fossil fuels are limited in output and quite expensive. The electric boat must have a method of storing electrical energy on board just as a fossil-fuel craft needs fuel in its tank, so batteries are as necessary as the motor. Cost, weight, capacity, replenishment characteristics, and cycle life are all important factors in building an appropriate battery bank.

ALTERNATIVES TO LEAD-ACID

Sad to say, the kind of battery powering today's electric boat is most likely the same type that powered electric boats 100 years ago. The lead-acid battery's low cost continues to make it the storage system of choice. Other electrical storage systems are available, and many new systems are in the experimental stages, but practicality must be our yardstick in evaluating these systems. Most electric-boat builders or owners have neither the need nor the necessary deep pockets for these sometimes exotic systems. Most experimental systems are directed toward developing viable land-based electric vehicles; fortunately, boats are a more accommodating platform for electric power. To evaluate alternative electrical storage systems, we can compare them with our sample 100-Ah 12-volt lead-acid battery.

The most obvious alternative to lead-acid is the nickel-cadmium battery. The NiCad battery is the most common rechargeable battery found around the house. The D-cells in the charger for the kids' toys, the power pack for portable shop tools, and the batteries in other rechargeable appliances and gadgets are all NiCads. It is interesting to note that the *Sun Seeker*, a PV-powered glider, worked its way across the continental U.S. using 96 D-cell NiCads for electrical storage.

NiCads have excellent cycling capability, can be deeply discharged without damage, and have good recharging characteristics. Replacing our 100-Ah lead-acid battery with a NiCad system gives us a battery bank with the following characteristics: It would weigh about 115 pounds versus 60 pounds for lead-acid, yielding an energy density of 10 Wh per pound compared with lead-acid's 20. The NiCad bank would be more than twice as large, occupying a volume of 1.2 cubic feet rather than the 0.47 cubic feet of the lead-acid battery. The cost of 100 Ah of NiCad capacity would be about $1,800 versus $80 for lead-acid. This last comparison is perhaps the decisive one; the life expectancy of the NiCad bank would have to be about 20 times that of lead-acid to justify the initial expense. Considering that the life-span of a well-cared-for lead-acid battery is in excess of four years, the NiCad would have to outlive the boatowner. And even with the slow rate at which new methods of storing electrical energy are being developed, something better than either NiCad or lead-acid is likely to be available within the next 80 years. So for all but a very few, NiCad systems can be ruled out as impractical for electric boats at this time. A number of other electrical storage systems are under close scrutiny, including zinc-air, sodium-sulfur, and chloride, but like NiCad, they're all currently impractical for use in electric boats. The lead-acid battery's proven and continued use in work vehicles such as forklifts, electric tugs, golf carts, and automobiles should not be taken lightly. From here on in this book, all energy storage systems discussed refer to lead-acid batteries. If a practical alternative presents itself at some future date, its substitution should present little problem.

THE OPEN-CELL LEAD-ACID BATTERY

The nature of lead-acid batteries has changed considerably over the years. One notable change is that they once were designed to be repaired or rebuilt, whereas now they are mostly disposed of or recycled for their metal when they fail. Not only are lead-acid batteries rarely rebuilt, but many batteries are now sealed to eliminate maintenance and inspection. The notion that a battery is a device that operates like magic and needs no attention is all too prevalent. A lead-acid battery is a working chemical machine that suffers from abuse and poor maintenance in the same way that a lawnmower or an automobile does. When you are in the middle of a big lake or many miles downriver from the hill, your battery is your best and perhaps your only friend. You should be aware of its condition and temperament, and treat it accordingly.

I have many pairs of jeans that became cutoffs courtesy of the lead–acid battery striking my leg while I was carrying it to and from the boat. This alone makes a good case for keeping the battery clean and exercising care in its transportation and maintenance. Even batteries that lie quietly below the sole demand frequent inspection to defeat the corrosive gremlin of battery acid.

How It Works

When two dissimilar metals—called the *positive* and *negative plates*—are immersed in an acid solution—called the *electrolyte*—a battery is created and a voltage developed. The amount of voltage depends on the types of metals and the electrolyte used.

The lead–acid battery stores and produces energy through a reversible chemical reaction involving lead dioxide and lead in an electrolyte medium of sulfuric acid. In a charged state, the positive plate consists primarily of lead dioxide and the negative plate of sponge lead. When the battery is connected to an external load, current flows and the discharge process begins. The lead dioxide of the positive plate is a compound of lead and oxygen; the sulfuric acid is a compound of hydrogen and the *sulfate radical*. As the battery discharges, the lead in the active material of the positive plate combines with the sulfate of the sulfuric acid to form lead sulfate on the positive plate, while the oxygen combines with hydrogen from the sulfuric acid to form water. A similar reaction occurs simultaneously at the negative plate: lead from the negative plate combines with sulfate from the sulfuric acid to form lead sulfate on the negative plate. During the discharge process, the sulfuric acid in the electrolyte is diluted with the water that is created as the hydrogen and oxygen combine, lowering the specific gravity of the electrolyte. Specific gravity is easily measured with a hydrometer, providing us with an accurate and convenient method for determining a battery's state of charge.

The chemical reactions that take place inside a charging battery are basically the reverse of those that occur during discharge.

Battery Construction

The plates inside a lead–acid battery are constructed on a plate grid made of an alloy of lead. The alloy sometimes contains small amounts of antimony to stiffen the soft lead for handling during manufacture, but reducing the antimony content and alloying with calcium or other metals reduces gassing, water usage, and self-discharge rates. The plate grid is the structural component of the plate and has cast in its structure the lugs for the electrical connections to combine a group of plates to form an element.

The plate grid is coated with a paste of lead oxide, sulfuric acid, and water, which has the consistency of firm mud. Other additives, such as fibers, help hold the material together. Expanders are required to prevent the negative material in the negative plate from contracting in service and reverting to a dense inactive state. Next the plates are given a forming charge while immersed in dilute sulfuric acid electrolyte. This charge electrochemically converts the lead oxide of the positive plate to lead dioxide, and the lead oxide of the negative plate to sponge lead.

Alternating positive and negative plates are stacked together, with separators between each plate. *Separators* are simply thin sheets of electrically insulating porous material used as spacers between the plates to prevent short circuits within the cells and still allow *ionic current flow*—the flow of electrically charged atoms or molecules— through the electrolyte between the positive and negative plates. A highly porous mat provides ample space for acid circulation and helps retain the active material.

Once the plates are stacked, the lugs of the negative plates are welded together, as are those of the positive plates, to form what is called an *element*. Any number of plates can make up an element, depending upon the desired performance. Installed in individual cells in a battery case, each element has an open-circuit voltage of approximately 2.1 volts and a current capacity proportional to the surface area of the plates. The elements can be combined as groups and connected by straps to produce batteries of different voltages. Six elements are required to make a 12-volt battery.

A container for these elements is constructed of hard rubber or plastic, molded in one piece and divided into the appropriate number of cells. The container is constructed to resist acid attack and mechanical shock, and an area is left open below each element to collect sediment shed from the plates. The one-piece cell cover has a vent well for each cell, generally with a ring or some other mark near its bottom to indicate the proper height to fill the cell when adding water or initially activating the battery. This level is usually ½ inch above the plates. Vent caps prevent electrolyte from being splashed from the cells or pumped out by escaping gas. Vent caps are available that reconstitute these gases to reduce water loss.

BATTERY RATINGS

Automobile batteries perform a function particular to their application. They are required to provide large cranking currents for a short period, after which they are immediately recharged by the automobile's alternator. They are subject to a shallow discharge of 2 to 5 percent of their capacity and normally operate in an 85- to 100-percent state of charge.

In contrast, electric-vehicle batteries are designed to accept deep discharges of 70 percent or more of their capacity. These batteries are referred to as *deep-cycle, deep-cycle-marine* (DCM), or most appropriately, *electric-vehicle* (EV) batteries. They are constructed with basically the same materials as described above but have thicker plates and additional reinforcement to prevent premature shedding of their active material.

Cold-cranking Amps

The *cold-cranking-amp* (CCA) rating generally applies to batteries intended for engine-starting applications, such as an automobile battery. CCA is defined as the discharge load in amps a battery at 0°F can deliver for 30 seconds and maintain a cell voltage of 1.2 volts or higher. A similar rating designated *marine cranking amp* (MCA) differs only in that the rating is at 32°F. The CCA rating usually falls between 300 and 600 amps for automobile batteries. This rating is not generally applied to EV batteries.

Reserve Capacity

Reserve capacity, or *reserve amp capacity* (RAC), is defined as the number of minutes a new, fully charged battery at 80°F can be discharged at 25 amps while maintaining a cell voltage of 1.75 volts. Reserve capacity may also be expressed for other rates of discharge, such as 5, 10, or 20 amps. Reserve capacity is the most universal battery rating and can be applied to EV batteries. If our sample battery could actually deliver 25 amps for 4 hours, the RAC rating would be 240 minutes.

Amp-Hours

In selecting a battery, we most often think of the *amp-hour rating*. Amp-hour rating is defined as the amps a battery can supply at 80°F for a specific amount of time—usually 20 hours in the U.S.—while maintaining a minimum cell voltage of 1.75. It is an indicator of the amount of usable electrical energy a battery can provide. Batteries perform differently at different discharge rates and should be selected on their ability to provide power efficiently at their expected load. For the amp-hour rating to be a true indicator of the actual performance we can expect, the variables of the rating in amps and time must be known. For example, while a standard 100-Ah battery is typically rated at 5 amps for 20 hours in the U.S., in the U.K. it will be rated at 10 amps for 10 hours, making the British battery actually more powerful than its American counterpart.

Battery ratings can be confusing because the way a battery is rated is largely determined by its intended use. While a CCA rating, for example, may be useful in selecting an automotive battery, we are far more interested in the amp-hour rating. If we buy a 100-Ah battery rated at 20 hours, we can expect it to supply 5 amps for the specified time, but will it also supply 25 amps for 4 hours? Probably not. A representative discharge curve (see graph on page 59) suggests that a 100-Ah-rated battery will actually supply 25 amps for a little over 2 hours. Running time, then, will depend greatly on our ability to operate our electric boat in the flatter, more efficient part of the discharge curve. Fortunately this is not difficult to accomplish in an electric boat.

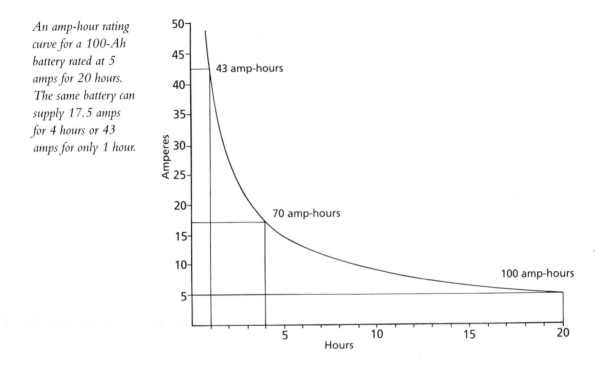

An amp-hour rating curve for a 100-Ah battery rated at 5 amps for 20 hours. The same battery can supply 17.5 amps for 4 hours or 43 amps for only 1 hour.

When basing a battery selection on amp-hours, it is essential to know what rate of discharge was used for the amp-hour rating. Some golf-cart batteries are referred to as 135-minute batteries. Years ago, while looking for a golf-cart motor, I asked the shop service man what this 135-minute rating meant to him. He looked at me as if I knew nothing at all about golf carts or batteries—he was half right, about the carts anyway—and told me it meant that a fully charged cart would run for 135 minutes at full power. I then asked him how many amp-hours this would equate to. His answer has stuck with me as one of those rare, unexpected truths we are lucky enough to pick up on occasion. "That's not important," he replied, "only the performance of the cart." In many respects this bit of wisdom applies to the selection of any battery bank; battery ratings can be used with great success for any application, but ultimately we will end up rating the bank on its actual performance.

Battery sizes, types, shapes, colors, and claims run from here to yonder, but one thing is uniformly common about lead-acid batteries: they are all heavy because they're made of lead. As a rule, the heavier the battery, the more power it will store.

SEALED LEAD-ACID BATTERIES

Sealed batteries, as the name implies, have no openings from which acid can spill or gases can escape. (Gases vented by charging batteries are flammable—even explosive in confined spaces.) They can be mounted in any position and almost any location, even inaccessibly since they never need added water and cannot be checked with a hydrometer to evaluate the state of charge. They typically contain more plates per element and in less space than regular lead-acid batteries, providing higher CCA ratings for their size.

There are currently two basic types of sealed lead-acid batteries: Absorbed-electrolyte batteries have closely spaced plates separated by electrolyte-saturated fiberglass and felt mat separators. In gel batteries, the electrolyte is in gel form. Because antimony in the plates is reduced or eliminated in favor of calcium or other metals, sealed batteries usually have low self-discharge rates, and they can handle higher charging and discharging rates.

The thin plates typically found in sealed batteries more closely resemble automotive-type batteries rather than DCM or EV batteries, however, suggesting fewer cycles and a shorter battery life than conventional thick-plate types. Unless you need the spill-proof and/or service-free nature of sealed batteries, you are likely to find that the open-cell lead-acid battery remains the choice in the battery banks of an electric boat. Still, advances in this technology certainly bear watching.

BATTERY LIFE

The number of discharge cycles specific batteries can deliver before they fail varies widely, even among batteries marketed for DCM and EV use. For example, the Surrette Battery Company has conducted laboratory tests of their top-of-the-line deep-cycle batteries that show a life of more than 2,500 cycles at 50-percent discharge. Such batteries are very expensive. So-called *marine batteries* from your local discount stores are more affordable, but they are also likely to deliver a tenth or less the number of cycles.

What battery you buy depends on how you plan to use and care for it. For example, if you go out in your electric canoe every weekend, discharging your battery once a week, even the least expensive deep-cycle battery should last four to five years. And if you fail to give an expensive battery proper care—keeping the water level up and maintaining a full charge—it won't last any longer than the cheap one. (For more on battery care, see page 70.)

Since changing batteries requires little effort and only modest expense in the kind of electric boats I use, I generally look for the best value (read "cheapest") deep-cycle battery I can find; but if I were building an electric launch, I would carefully investigate the various batteries available and try to buy units that would give 10 or 20 years of service before requiring replacement. Next to motor selection, battery selection is the electric boater's most important decision.

CHAPTER 7

BUILDING AND MAINTAINING A BATTERY BANK

THE BATTERY BANK can constitute half the weight of an electric boat. The size and configuration of the battery bank depend upon the various factors discussed in previous chapters. Building a battery bank appropriate for an electric boat may require not only the consideration of speed and range but also overland transportation, onboard power sources, and auxiliary electrical equipment.

Few large electric boats spend a lot of time on the highway. They are usually at their moorings being charged or awaiting the next opportunity to serve. It they are transported overland, their batteries may or may not remain aboard. In the case of small boats that are cartopped or carried on a truck bed, the batteries are rarely left on board. Not only does this make the boat easier to load and unload, but it keeps the fragile batteries from being jostled about in the empty hull.

Batteries that are removed from the boat on a regular basis for charging or transport should be small enough to be easy to handle, have a carrying strap, and be sturdily constructed.

ONBOARD POWER SOURCES

In a hybrid craft—an electric boat capable of generating its own power—a fossil-fuel-powered generator could significantly reduce the size of the battery bank. The key word here is *could*. The purpose of a generator aboard an electric boat is usually to extend the craft's range by providing recharging capabilities when away from the grid. But the design purpose of the electric boat is easily defeated in a hybrid craft since the amount of time the generator will need to run is likely to be about the same as the running time of the boat, given that a well-chosen battery bank in an electric craft will generally take about as long to recharge as to deplete in normal use. For a hybrid boat to function with the quiet characteristics of an electric boat using stored power only, the addition of the generator should not lead to any reduction in the size of the battery bank.

The need for stored capacity can be reduced without compromising the electric-boat concept through extensive use of photovoltaics. The difference between photovoltaics and the fossil-fuel generator centers on two outstanding features of the PV panel: it works all the time the sun is shining, and it's silent. A significant PV array, coupled with the usually conservative nature of the PV-power enthusiast, could allow for a substantial reduction in reserve capacity.

A large electric boat that routinely exceeds its energy reserve likely has the option of increasing the size of its battery bank or, if the excess demand is a temporary condition, of simply taking aboard additional batteries. These options are not always open to the smaller craft. An extended outing of several days in an electric canoe, for example, requires either battery swaps or stops at recharging stations along the way since the canoe will be unable to carry on board the electrical energy necessary for the entire trip. A third solution is to carry along a portable gas-powered charger (see photo on bottom of page 6). The charger in this application, with fuel for several days, weighs less than 25 pounds.

Onboard power sources can and in some cases do affect reserve capacity, but in considering this option, one should keep in mind that the underlying purpose of the electric boat is to afford its occupants a quiet and clean outing.

SPEED AND RANGE

Speed and range are the main criteria in determining reserve capacity. In Chapter 3, we established that 1 h.p. is equal to about 750 watts, meaning that the electrical power required to run a 1-h.p. electric boat is about 750 watts at top speed (full power). Though most electric boats are rarely operated at full power for long periods, a reasonable expectation of the electrical energy to be used could still be based on total horsepower available and time of use. An electric boat equipped with a 3-h.p. motor would need 2,250 watts at top speed, but actual power use would probably average 50 percent or less of full power, or 1.5 h.p.

It is very important to have full power available even if it's rarely used. For example, for a contrary current of 2 mph or an equivalent resistance in wind encountered on an open lake, the most efficient use of power is to traverse this area as quickly as possible and then resume a lower speed. An electric canoe traveling upstream against a current has to exceed the speed of the current; at the same time, its energy consumption has to be monitored to make the best use of its battery bank. In this case the boatspeed required probably would be less than full power but still a comfortable margin above current speed. These judgment calls are the captain's, and they represent a challenge in energy planning and use that the operator of a fossil-fuel outboard seldom has to face. For me, these are the most challenging exercises in operating an electric boat.

My uncle Luther and I went upriver one pleasant February afternoon years back, each of us using a Guide. My boat had a fresh 100-Ah battery, and Luther was using an 85-Ah battery with a little age on it. I took the stronger battery for myself so that if we ran low on power, I could tie the two boats at the points and carry us both home. This is a common practice even if both boats enjoy good reserves because it allows one of the operators complete freedom from steering and puts the travelers side by side.

This was Luther's first time out as captain of an electric boat, and I gave him pointers as we proceeded upriver. Within the first hour he appeared to have mastered the little boat and was enjoying the outing. I knew our destination approached the limit of our range, and we would have to rely on the current to bring us back, using our depleted reserves only for control. Luther liked going fast, but I cautioned him to slow down and save his power.

We reached our destination without incident, and after warming in the sun, we slipped quietly off the white sand for the downriver trip back home. As expected, my reserves were low and Luther's even lower. I encouraged Luther to go slowly and choose his moves carefully.

Maximum power is more important going downstream than up because downstream you are traveling at current speed plus boatspeed. I knew that decisions to avoid overhanging trees or sleepers must be made quickly; evasive action takes ample power.

No sooner had these thoughts crossed my mind than I saw Luther being pushed under a low-hanging ironwood. Without the power necessary to steer to safety, within seconds he was washed broadside into the branches. My suggestion to lie flat and be still was lost in the excitement of the moment. Instead, he grabbed a tree limb, giving life to my worst fears. The Guide whisked my uncle into the water as quickly as you would flick a bug off your forearm, only to right itself and proceed downriver unencumbered by its rider.

I mention this episode to make three points: Expecting full power and not having it can spell disaster. In the event of finding yourself with lower reserves than you need, you should know what to expect. And don't be grabbing at tree limbs.

To determine the size of a battery bank, we need to look at three reserve levels. A full bank will operate at full power for a specified length of time—in this case 4 hours. An average bank will provide 50 percent of full power for the same length of time but have the capacity to perform at full power on occasion. A barebones bank will also operate at 50 percent of full power for the specified time, but leaves the reserve fully depleted at the end. Banks will be made up of open-cell lead-acid EV (or deep-cycle) batteries.

DISCHARGE RATE AND CAPACITY

A battery or bank of batteries performs most efficiently when discharged at a low rate. This contributes to the increased range electric boats may achieve by reducing speed and corresponding power consumption. Our 100-Ah battery starts to drop off in efficiency when pressed to deliver more than 20 amps per hour (see graph on page 58). Applying this performance curve to configuring an efficient bank, we can conclude that power demand should not exceed 20 percent of rated capacity. Our 0.4-h.p. motor requires 25 amps at 12 volts, so in this case, the minimum bank capacity indicated is 125 amps.

$$25 \text{ amps}/0.2 = 125 \text{ amps}$$

For a 4-hour range, the total amp-hours used at full power is 100. But batteries give up their energy begrudgingly at the lower limits of their capacity, and the boat slows down long before it stops. As Uncle Luther discovered, we need to maintain the ability to operate at full power at any time, and this isn't possible when tapping those last few amps.

We will use 70 percent of capacity as the discharge limit for our battery bank. Battery-cycle life can be improved if we limit discharge to 50 percent of capacity, but this also greatly increases the system's mass. Since we are stressing the battery bank, good maintenance and charging practices are essential to extending the cycle life. Limiting the discharge to 70 percent of capacity, we need a battery reserve of 143 Ah for 4 hours of full-power operation.

$$25 \text{ amps} \times 4 \text{ hours}/0.7 = 143 \text{ amp-hours}$$

This is the full-bank reserve level. This much capacity puts the 25-amp draw within the efficient area of the discharge curve, although near the edge, and should yield ample range at low levels of power usage.

Larger boats are generally more efficient than our sample, but it still may be interesting to determine the full-bank reserves suggested by these numbers for boats with 1 h.p. or larger motors. To avoid limiting our results to 12-volt systems (not generally found on larger boats), we can perform the calculations in watts rather than amps.

We already know that the power required to drive 1 h.p. is 750 watts, without regard to voltage. If this power demand is not to exceed 20 percent of reserves, the total power of our battery bank cannot be less than 3,750 watts.

$$750 \text{ watts}/0.2 = 3,750 \text{ watts}$$

However, we want 4 hours of full-power operation, limiting discharge to 70 percent of capacity. This means our energy requirement will be 4,286 Wh.

$$750 \text{ watts} \times 4 \text{ hours}/0.7 = 4,286 \text{ watt-hours}$$

We can see that use-time, not peak demand, is the determining factor for bank size, given a typical use pattern and a 70 percent limitation on discharge. This discharge limitation also keeps us in the acceptable range of the discharge curve.

If we know the voltage of our system, we can convert our watt-hour requirement into amp-hours. For the purpose of illustration, let's make this calculation for four possible voltages.

$$4,286 \text{ watt-hours}/12 \text{ volts} = 357 \text{ amp-hours}$$
$$4,286 \text{ watt-hours}/24 \text{ volts} = 179 \text{ amp-hours}$$
$$4,286 \text{ watt-hours}/36 \text{ volts} = 119 \text{ amp-hours}$$
$$4,286 \text{ watt-hours}/48 \text{ volts} = 89 \text{ amp-hours}$$

These values, then, are the amp-hour requirements per horsepower—depending on system voltage—for 4 hours of full-power operation with a maximum discharge of 70 percent.

Commercially available electric pleasure craft carrying six or so passengers typically rely on a 3-h.p. motor to achieve top speed. A full bank for a 3-h.p. 36-volt motor requires 357 Ah of battery capacity.

$$119 \text{ amp-hours per horsepower} \times 3 \text{ horsepower} =$$
$$357 \text{ amp-hours (at 36 volts)}$$

If the bank is to be made up of 6-volt batteries—a common practice—six batteries, each with 357 Ah of capacity, must be connected in series. When batteries are connected in series, only the potential, or voltage, increases; the amperage is unchanged; i.e., the total current capacity of a series-connected bank of batteries is the same as that of each individual battery, just at a higher voltage. The opposite is true when the batteries are connected in parallel: current capacities are added and the voltage remains the same.

Using a standard 220-Ah 6-volt battery (the ubiquitous golf-cart battery), we will need 2 batteries in parallel to meet our current requirement—giving us 440 Ah of capacity. To satisfy our voltage requirement—36 volts—we need to connect 6 of these battery pairs in series for a bank total of 12 batteries. Most boats in this power range carry half this reserve, which indicates that they are rarely operated at full speed for long periods. Our suggested battery bank will weigh 792 pounds and cost about $1,584.

In practice, the ideal bank for optimum battery-cycle life giving a true range of 4 hours at top speed without discharging below 30 percent capacity is often considered unnecessary. Basing our calculations on 100-percent discharge and half power, or 1.5 h.p., gives us a bare-bones bank for 4 hours of operation of 4,500 Wh.

1.5 horsepower x 750 watts per horsepower × 4 hours = 4,500 watt-hours
4,500 watt-hours/36 volts = 125 amp-hours

Such a bare-bones bank would suffer from frequent deep discharges of the six series-connected 125-Ah 6-volt batteries. It would take the motor hours to suck up those last amps while pushing the boat at a snail's pace—and shortening battery life. If we apply the 20-percent-of-capacity rule for maximum demand against this bank for full 3-h.p. operation, we find the total capacity is inadequate.

3 horsepower × 750 watts per horsepower = 2,250 watts
2,250 watts/36 volts = 63 amps

Instead of 20 percent, full-power operation demands 50 percent of reserve capacity, operating in a very inefficient and possibly damaging range of our battery's capability. While we may safely exceed the 20-percent limitation if full-power operation is brief and infrequent, demand should never exceed 40 percent of rated capacity.

To determine the capacity for an average battery bank, we want to be able to operate at 50 percent of full power for 4 hours.

119 amp-hours per horsepower × 1.5 horsepower =
178.5 amp-hours (at 36 volts)

(Note that peak demand will be above the recommended limitation of 20 percent but below the 40-percent limitation for short-duration use.)

This calls for a bank of six 179-Ah 6-volt batteries. Instead, we would likely use six standard 220-Ah 6-volt batteries, which would provide ample capacity at a convenient unit size. Alternative configurations could consist of three 180-Ah 12-volt batteries or six 90-Ah 12-volt batteries. In most cases, battery banks utilize standard batteries for reasons of economy and size. Because of problems in matching electric potentials, all the batteries in a bank should be the same type, age, and capacity.

THE CHARGING CYCLE

Battery charging isn't always a simple matter; battery banks are not all the same size. The simplest bank is a single battery, like the sample 100-Ah 12-volt battery powering our example electric canoe, but even this "bank" is made up of cells, or elements, each with a potential of about 2.1 volts. The capacity in amps is determined by the amount of material in the cell, specifically the total surface area of the plates making up the element. These two factors in some combination make up every bank. Most banks are made up of a group of cells in what we usually think of as a battery, such as our 12-volt sample. The point here is that every bank of any configuration is made up of some number of cells. Each of these cells is an individual entity, and to understand a battery bank is to understand the single cell.

Recharging is generally an attempt to bring each cell to its fully charged condition. This would be quite simple if each cell could be charged individually, but this is rarely the case. Cells are instead charged in groups as a single battery—such as our 100-Ah sample—or in a bank of batteries. Therefore, chargers and charging systems need to be designed for the depth (amps) and potential (volts) for each particular bank.

Knowing the State of Charge

The most accurate method of determining the state of charge of a lead-acid battery is to test the specific gravity of its cells using a standard hydrometer. Not only will we learn the state of charge of each cell, but we will also find out which of the cells might be weak. If proper treatment using an equalizing charge (discussed later) cannot bring a weak cell in line with the others, then the cell should be replaced. Of course, today's batteries are rarely repairable, so a weak cell actually leads to the replacement of the entire battery.

Another method of determining the state of charge is to measure the open-circuit voltage. Since the change in voltage from full charge to "dead" is only about 1 volt, evaluating battery condition from voltage requires a precise reading. In the

An ordinary 10-amp battery charger. (Photo courtesy Advantage Auto Stores)

BUILDING A BATTERY BANK

case of sealed batteries, this is the only practical method of determining state of charge. Some batteries have a built-in float indicator in one of the cells that reacts to changes in specific gravity to give a visual indication of the state of charge.

Charging

In some ways battery charging and discharging are similar, both involving a reversible chemical reaction. The speed of both reactions is a function of ion flow through the electrolyte, which is in turn affected by temperature and the rate of charge or discharge. The rule of thumb is that most batteries will accept a charge at about the same rate as they can be safely discharged. Deep-cycle batteries typically operate between 30 percent and 90 percent of their capacities; to extend battery life, we choose not to discharge the battery below 30 percent, and the low charge rate required to "top off" the final 10 percent of a near-fully charged battery is often perceived as not worth the effort.

On the water in our electrically propelled boat, our power usage should be conservative, but this doesn't have to be the case in charging. Usually we want the batteries recharged as quickly as possible without damage to the system.

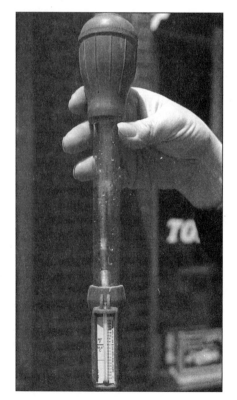

A hydrometer for checking battery condition.

Our 100–Ah battery in a 70-percent-discharged state should easily accept a charge current of at least 40 amps at a voltage of 13.8 or more. This voltage is required to overcome the battery voltage, which even at this depth of discharge is about 12.2 volts, and the battery's internal resistance. Like water, electricity flows to its lowest potential.

As the charging battery reaches about half its capacity, the charging current should be reduced to about half the balance of its capacity—in this case to 25 amps. This halving procedure should ideally continue until the battery is fully charged. The last 5 percent or so of charge requires a long time at a low current of 2.5

amps. It is not economical to use a generator for this purpose.

Batteries in the 90-percent-charged state are good candidates for photovoltaics or trickle chargers with an output of about 13.2 to 13.6 volts. These provide what is often referred to as a *float charge*. When a battery reaches the float cycle, it is no longer accepting a large amount of power regardless of the capacity of the charging source, and to increase current to such a battery by raising the charging voltage is to chance damage, especially if it's a sealed battery.

During charging, battery gassing and heating occurs, and this usually results in water loss. All cells should be checked before the charging process is started to make sure the plates are covered with water, and the cells should be topped off when charging is complete.

Open-cell liquid-electrolyte batteries may be *equalized*, or gassed, by subjecting the fully charged battery to a constant current of 3 or 4 amps for a few hours. This procedure equalizes the specific gravity of each cell, assuring that each cell is fully charged. A battery being equalized should be gassing freely, and close monitoring of electrolyte level and battery temperature is advisable.

TABLE 7-1. DETERMINING STATE OF CHARGE BY
MEASURING SPECIFIC GRAVITY OF SINGLE CELLS

Depth of Discharge in Percent	Specific Gravity at 77°F	Volts per Cell	12 Volt (Nominal)	24 Volt (Nominal)
0	1.266	2.106	12.63	25.27
10	1.251	2.091	12.54	25.09
20	1.236	2.076	12.45	24.91
30	1.221	2.061	12.36	24.73
40	1.206	2.046	12.27	24.55
50	1.191	2.031	12.18	24.37
60	1.176	2.016	12.09	24.19
70	1.161	2.001	12.00	24.01
80	1.146	1.985	11.91	23.83
90	1.131	1.971	11.82	23.65

Battery gases consist primarily of hydrogen, which is extremely flammable and explosive in close quarters. Hydrogen has the highest ignition velocity of any flammable gas and, being environmentally friendly, makes an excellent rocket fuel but should not be welcome in the hold of a boat. Ensure that there is adequate ventilation.

BUILDING A BATTERY BANK

Charge Controllers

Equalizing is an example of *constant current charging*. Constant current is best used (at a low current level) to maintain a battery at its full charge level. *Constant potential charging,* on the other hand, allows the battery to accept a maximum amount of current at a constant voltage. The typical charging voltage for an automobile battery is about 13.8 volts. This allows for a good rate of recharge of a shallowly discharged battery. A deeply discharged battery could be charged more rapidly at a higher initial voltage setting and later floated at a lower level. More sophisticated charge controllers provide this variation of potential for maximum charging. In most cases the idea behind such controllers is to recharge as quickly as possible to reduce the required running time of the alternator—and the engine that drives it. This might not be of particular concern where power from the grid is being used and time is not a factor.

EFFECTS OF TEMPERATURE

It is important to note that battery performance is rated at 80°F and that storage and charging characteristics change at very low temperatures. Batteries require higher charge voltages at lower temperatures. At 0°F a completely discharged battery is in danger of freezing and should not be recharged before warming.

Low temperatures reduce the chemical reaction in a battery's cells. At 0°F a battery's capacity may be reduced as much as 60 percent. Although this is more a factor in automobile starting batteries than in EV batteries, it is still important to be aware of the need for temperature corrections to hydrometer readings and possible adjustments to charging regulators.

Battery banks might need to be increased in size in particularly cold environments. Conversely, a battery bank could be downsized in a tropical operating environment.

BATTERY CARE

An open-cell lead-acid battery should be recharged as soon after use as possible, preferably within 24 hours. If left deeply discharged for a long time, the plates become sulfated and the battery will be difficult if not impossible to bring back to its full capacity.

Resurrecting a sulfated battery involves providing low currents over a period of days. Additives such as ethylenediamine tetraacetic acid, or EDTA—available at some autoparts stores—can help revive sulfated batteries. Use one or two teaspoons per 100 Ah of capacity, dissolved in water and added to each cell, followed by extended charging. Adding anything other than distilled water to a battery in good condition is never good policy. But a sulfated battery *isn't* a good battery but one that is dead to the world and destined for the salvage yard. No harm giving it a try; just suit up and be careful around the acid lest it make rags of your trousers.

My charger is an automobile alternator belted to an old washing machine motor. It isn't fancy and might not be as economical to operate as a new unit, but it was cheap to build and really puts out the juice. If you're not so fortunate as to have a couple of old junkers in the back pasture, I don't recommend buying these parts new. A tapering charger or a PV panel is a better investment. If you do have access to an old alternator and its regulator, and a motor of a half-horse or better, it may be worthwhile to put them together. The motor can even be a part of another machine that is idle when the parent machine is not in use. For many years I used the motor on my drum sander with the alternator mounted inconspicuously below with great success—until another motor turned up in salvage. If you have an old-fashioned electromechanical regulator whose voltage setting can be altered, I suggest setting it to about 15 volts for a 12-volt EV battery. Keep a close eye on the battery's state of charge.

A simple motor-generator set made from salvaged parts and good for 30 amps at 12 volts DC.

The battery is a chemical engine, your lead-acid man, the most used and active part of the electric boat. It should be fed and groomed in a caring manner. Ride it hard and put it up hungry, and all too soon it will be dead.

CHAPTER 8

PUTTING IT TOGETHER

THE MOST IMPORTANT THINGS a designer needs to know are the environment in which a boat is to be used, including size restrictions and speed requirements; the load it is expected to carry; and the desired range.

Environmental considerations could be expanded to include the type of weather and water conditions expected and the comforts and luxury afforded the occupants, but the real concern is with the nature of the water the boat will see in service. These questions must be addressed: How deep is the run? If currents are involved, how fast are they? Will underwater obstructions be common? Is overhead clearance a factor? How about wind? All these factors taken together define a boat's purpose, and thus its design.

Years ago I set about to build an electric boat that would carry me from my shop about 100 miles downriver to the ocean. The water depth ranged from almost none to plenty. Where the river opens up near the sea there would be wind to contend with. There would be currents to travel against and boat wakes to breast. The boat was to be carried in the bed of a pickup truck and have the capacity to carry two people with gear. This was its design purpose.

Najas was in every sense a dreamboat, consuming my days in the shop as well as that most productive time just before sleep overtakes the mind. I even had to borrow money, not so much to pay for the boat—it was wood—but to pay for the time. But when it was time for *Najas*'s first show at the Maritime Museum at Beaufort, North Carolina, it tied for top and only honors with *Silver Chalice*, a boat the Museum had built. I showed the boat once more, in South Carolina, and it

Elco luxury. The interior of an 1898, 30-foot Electric Fantail Launch. (Photo courtesy Elco)

won best in class. After that, *Najas* retired to the river where it was most at home.

Najas filled its design requirements, won awards, and had the unanticipated effect of an invitation to write this book. Designing and building this unique boat was a great learning experience, and I will share with you the lessons learned.

The problem of range for an electric boat can best be solved by having an onboard generator. The generator aboard *Najas* was completely portable and, at 19

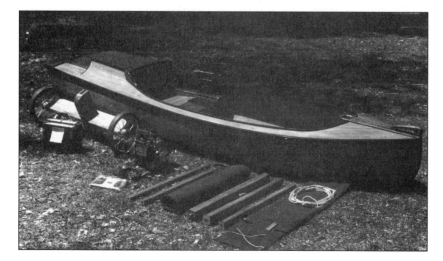

Najas *with all components, including dolly.*

pounds, presented few problems. To further enhance the boat's range, a spritsail was rigged, with a mast and boom that could be broken down and stowed away. The hull was 12 feet long and 32 inches wide and was propelled by a 0.4-h.p. electric submersible mounted in a tunnel, allowing an 8-inch draft. Power was stored in a single 85-Ah battery. The boat was strip-built of salvaged white cedar and black walnut, finished bright.

Najas could do all the things it was designed to do, but it did no one thing exceptionally well except please the crowds who saw it. Even empty of its components, it was difficult to load onto the truck. The generator could carry the boat if the battery was down, but it stank and sounded like a chain saw in a breadbox. The sail was fun downwind, but because of the shallow draft requirement the boat had little keel, so windward performance was marginal. It did perform well in the shallows, but because of its loaded weight, it was difficult to drag across snags. Soon, outings on the river rarely exceeded a single day, and I often found myself taking a simpler boat with one good battery. *Najas* was quickly becoming a shop ornament.

I mention *Najas* to bring home the importance of the design purpose. Keep it simple. Ask of the design only what is necessary and don't try to do too much. Simplicity is the key to any good idea—including a good electric boat.

DEEP DRAFT . . .

The first portion of an electric boat to strike bottom is usually the propeller or, if so equipped, the skeg, which is there to protect the prop from just such an event. Thus, propeller size and hull draft determine the depth of the water in which a boat can successfully operate. In most lakes and some estuaries, draft is no problem, and your propeller of choice will probably be large and slow-turning, which means efficient, quiet operation. A boat for deep water can also be large and heavy, allowing greater flexibility in accommodations and power reserve. Included in this class of craft are electric launches or pleasure boats with propeller diameters from 12 to 20 inches or greater and shaft speeds of 300 to 1,100 rpm. Of course, smaller propellers or even jets could be used in these waters, but at the expense of efficiency and quiet operation.

Turning a large propeller to good effect requires an equally large motor. An electric launch is likely to need from 1 to 5 h.p. Motors at the low end of this range may be the permanent-magnet type, with larger motors almost always being field-wound. Motor speed will be from 1,100 to 3,100 rpm, usually delivered to the propeller shaft via a gear or belt system with a 2:1 to 10:1 reduction ratio. The diameter and pitch of the propeller will depend on the power to be delivered, shaft rpm, and boatspeed. Most electric propulsion systems in this horsepower range are inboard with rudder steering, but there are some U.S.-made submersibles that

*The Ray Electric
3.5-h.p. outboard.
(Photo courtesy
Ray Electric)*

approach 1 h.p. and some above-water electric outboards that are well up in the range.

Craft of this size usually adopt most new accessories and innovations. Speed control will be variable, reserve electrical capacity ample, and the boat will be equipped with an onboard charger that can be plugged into a standard outlet at dockside. These pleasure boats are most at home on the lake or at the dock. They represent the owner in the manner he wishes to be seen—and rather lavishly so, more often than not. As maximum range may be of less significance than comfort, their hull shapes trade speed and range for beam and ballast stability.

. . . AND SHALLOW

The shallow waters of rivers, creeks, and swamps present an entirely different environment to the electric boat. The purpose of the outing changes from a primarily social function to a more intimate relationship with nature. Here a boat may see extended stretches of water where a foot of depth is considered adequate and where snags, sandbars, and other obstacles must be considered part of the trip. Though boats for this environment can be fairly large, they are usually relatively small—most like canoes.

The very nature of traveling in shallow water requires a trade-off in accommodations and design efficiencies. The first thing to suffer is propeller size, with a resultant loss in efficiency. Smaller propellers require an increase in shaft speed with a concomitant increase in noise. Small props are the realm of the submersible motor.

Sometimes the motor is fixed in a tunnel and the boat steered by a rudder, but more often the motor rotates on its mounting shaft to provide steering. In many applications the motor is simply an electric outboard of either the above-water or submersible variety.

Low-hanging branches, shallow water, and other obstacles make the electric canoe a good choice for backwater exploring.

A trolling motor modified for use on a small fishing boat. (Photo courtesy Crow Boats)

Propeller sizes and blade configurations vary quite a bit among submersibles, each propeller having its own advantages. As submersibles usually do not exceed 0.5 h.p., they lack the power to turn large propellers at their effective operating rpm. Some submersibles and all above-water outboards reduce the propeller-shaft rpm. Combined with a larger prop, this does allow for greater efficiency, but it may also increase draft. Propellers for submersible and above-water electric outboards range from 6 to 12 inches in diameter and come in two-, three-, and four-blade configurations. Shaft speeds generally range from 800 to 1,500 rpm.

The electric canoe or kayak is typically powered by a submersible steered by mounting-shaft rotation. This configuration in a short, beamy boat makes for a close turning radius, fair draft, and unimpressive cruising speeds. In longer, narrower boats better speeds can be maintained with a moderate loss in turning capability. A good electric canoe should be able to operate in 12 inches of water or less and have the ability to skip over obstacles at half that depth by virtue of a well-protected propeller and adequate rocker (see Chapter 9). Protecting the propeller is usually accomplished by tunnel-mounting or with a well-made skeg (see photo on facing page).

An ordinary submersible trolling motor mounted in a small boat without a transom mount. Protected by a skeg, the motor rotates on the mounting shaft to steer—much like an inboard-outboard.

Since an electric canoe with batteries aboard usually weighs as much as 220 pounds, it should be tough enough to be dragged across debris or shallows. It should have good speed, both for efficiency and for making headway against fast currents. Electrical storage can be a standard 100-Ah 12-volt battery, or the boat can be given more capacity if the intended range or the demands of a particular outing require it. When empty and without the batteries aboard, it can be cartopped or carried in a truck bed, avoiding the necessity of a trailer.

The electric canoe is perhaps the most rugged of electric craft. Because it is likely to see more hard use than its larger pleasure-boat relatives, attention to its design and mechanical worthiness is of great importance, followed closely by considerations of comfort and accommodations.

RANGE

The range of an electric boat is largely a function of the electrical capacity on board, which in most cases is electrical energy stored in batteries. Photovoltaics and onboard generators can extend range, but the cost of these can be difficult to justify considering the low cost of replenishment from the grid.

Good range requires an efficient hull. The well-used formula for determining the "hull speed"—the maximum speed of a displacement hull in ordinary conditions—is:

$$\text{Hull speed in knots} = 1.34 \times \sqrt{(WL)}$$
where
$$WL = \text{waterline length in feet}$$

Using this formula, we find that we can expect a displacement hull 16 feet long to operate efficiently at speeds up to 5.36 knots. Converting to mph—1 knot = 1.15 mph—gives us a hull speed of 6.2 mph. Applying the same formula to a 30-foot hull gives us a hull speed of 7.34 knots, or 8.4 mph. Most boats suitable for electric propulsion fall somewhere between these two lengths—and speeds.

Having established what can reasonably be expected from our hull, we need to determine the power required to achieve this speed. We do this by using the following formula from Dave Gerr's *Propeller Handbook:*

$$\text{S/L ratio} = 10.665/\sqrt[3]{(\text{LB/SHP})}$$

where

S/L (speed/length) ratio = $\text{Kts}/\sqrt{(\text{WL})}$
LB = displacement in pounds
SHP = shaft horsepower at the propeller
Kts = boat speed in knots

Plugging the numbers for our 16-foot canoe into this formula—assuming a displacement (including a 280-pound payload) of 500 pounds—we find that we need 1 h.p. to achieve 5.36 knots (6.2 mph).

$$\text{Kts}/\sqrt{(\text{WL})} = 10.665/\sqrt[3]{(\text{LB/SHP})}$$
$$5.36/\sqrt{(16)} = 10.665/\sqrt[3]{(500/\text{SHP})}$$
$$\text{SHP} = 1 \text{ horsepower}$$

Doing the same calculations for a boat with a 30-foot waterline and a displacement of 5,000 pounds, we arrive at a 10-h.p. power requirement to achieve a speed of 7.34 knots (8.4 mph).

$$7.34/\sqrt{(30)} = 10.655/\sqrt[3]{(5,000/\text{SHP})}$$
$$\text{SHP} = 10 \text{ horsepower}$$

In both cases, most electric boats will have only about half these indicated power requirements, so these boats will be unable to reach hull speed in normal conditions. How fast will they go?

Solving for a number of S/L ratios, not just the one representing hull speed, we can get an array of horsepower requirements, which are reduced to pounds per horsepower and plotted as the curve in the accompanying graph.

From the graph, we can see that pushing our 500-pound canoe with a 0.5-h.p. motor gives us a pound per horsepower value of 1,000, so the S/L ratio we are operating at is about 1.07. We can calculate this value as well.

$$\text{S/L ratio} = 10.655/\sqrt[3]{(500/0.5)} = 1.07$$

This gives a 16-foot waterline boat displacing 500 pounds a speed of about 5 mph.

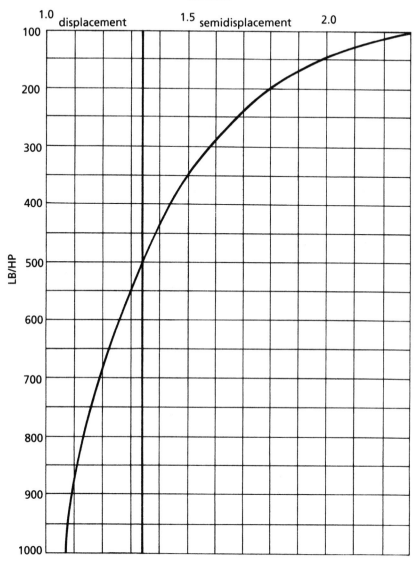

S/L Ratio

This curve represents the relationship between shaft horsepower (SHP), displacement, and the speed/length ratio. The chart shows the power necessary to achieve a specific speed/length ratio. The vertical line represents the practical speed limitation—hull speed—for displacement hulls.

$$\text{S/L ratio} = \text{Kts}/\sqrt{(\text{WL})} \quad \text{or} \quad \text{Kts} = \text{S/L ratio} \times \sqrt{(\text{WL})}$$
$$\text{Kts} = 1.07 \times \sqrt{(16)} = 4.28 \text{ knots or } 4.9 \text{ mph}$$

We can do similar calculations for the 30-foot, 5,000-pound vessel, which will give us a speed of about 7 mph. With energy at such a premium on an electric boat, it is easy to see that giving up 1 mph to reduce power consumption by 50 percent is an easy trade.

Keep in mind that both length and displacement determine how efficiently an electric boat uses the power available. For example, a very light (300 pounds) and long (21 feet) electric boat powered with the same 0.5-h.p. motor as our 16-foot canoe would operate at an S/L ratio of almost 1.3 and be capable of a speed of about 6.7 mph.

$$\text{S/L ratio} = 10.655/\sqrt[3]{(300/0.5)} = 1.26$$
$$\text{Speed} = 1.26 \times \sqrt{(21)} = 5.79 \text{ knots or } 6.66 \text{ mph}$$

With our conservative power requirements established, we now need to calculate the necessary power storage for the desired range in miles. Powering the 0.5-h.p. motor in our 16-foot vessel at full speed—about 5 mph—requires 375 watts.

$$0.5 \text{ horsepower} \times 750 \text{ watts per horsepower} = 375 \text{ watts}$$

We can use this value to calculate the size of the battery bank we will need to achieve a particular range. For example, a fast 20-mile run in our electric canoe will require 4 hours. That translates into 1,500 Wh (375 watts × 4 hours) of available energy; i.e., a battery bank with at least 125 Ah of usable capacity.

We can just as easily determine the range of the battery bank our electric boat already has. If we give our electric canoe a pair of 100-Ah 12-volt batteries, we have 2,400 Wh of energy aboard.

$$200 \text{ amp-hours} \times 12 \text{ volts} = 2,400 \text{ watt-hours}$$

We can calculate the range to be about 6.4 hours and 32 miles of full-speed operation.

$$2,400 \text{ watt-hours}/375 \text{ watts} = 6.4 \text{ hours}$$
$$6.4 \text{ hours} \times 5 \text{ mph} = 32 \text{ miles}$$

Unfortunately, we haven't yet taken into consideration the need to limit our discharge to 70 percent of total capacity, so the actual full-speed range will be about 22 miles. Of course, slowing down will give us a more efficient S/L ratio and extend our range substantially.

In the previous chapter we determined that the per-horsepower reserve requirement for 4 hours of full-power operation, limiting discharge to 70 percent, was 4,286 Wh. Equipped with a 5-h.p. motor, our 5,000-pound displacement, 30-foot waterline electric boat would carry a battery bank with 21,430 Wh of storage capacity. Such a craft should have a full-speed (7 mph) range of about 5.7 hours, traveling 40 miles.

$$5 \text{ horsepower} \times 750 \text{ watts per horsepower} = 3,750 \text{ watts}$$

$$21,430 \text{ watt-hours}/3,750 \text{ watts} = 5.7 \text{ hours}$$
$$5.7 \text{ hours} \times 7 \text{ mph} = 39.9 \text{ miles}$$

Holding the depth of discharge to 70 percent, actual range would be about 28 miles. Given good lines, a large propeller, and deep, unobstructed water, an electric launch doesn't suffer the efficiency losses inherent in the electric canoe and should achieve the calculated range.

Range can always be increased with a larger battery bank or the addition of a generator or solar panels. This is especially true for larger boats, where ballast can be easily replaced with additional batteries, and there is ample space or carrying capacity for solar arrays or a generator. For practical purposes, however, outing times usually don't exceed the 5 to 7 hours we've calculated, especially at top speed. As speed is reduced, the overall efficiency rises sharply, and we can expect greater ranges and longer potential running time.

EXTENDED RANGE

Extending the range of an electric boat beyond that of its stored energy requires electrical replenishment through recharging—either on board or at some station— or battery replacement; or it requires another source of propulsion such as sail, paddle, or heat engine. As these latter means could function as the primary power source, we will not consider them as viable options for a true electric boat. Instead, let's look at more appropriate ways to extend the range of an electric boat without increasing the size of the battery bank. We begin with the fossil-fuel-powered electric generator.

Generators

Onboard generators are not that common on electric vessels but are sometimes listed as options. Common sense suggests that a gallon of gasoline converted directly into forward thrust by a small gas outboard is more efficient than that same gallon used to run an engine to spin a generator to recharge a battery to power an electric motor to spin a propeller. Still, a gasoline- or diesel-powered onboard generator is one method of extending the range of an electric boat. This range increase is directly proportional to the amount of fuel carried on board to power the generator. Unfortunately, this option also blurs the distinction between our boat and fossil-fuel inboard or outboard craft, introducing some characteristics that are at cross-purposes with the electrically propelled vessel.

Looking back to our 16-footer, let's examine the effect of adding a gasoline generator. We already know that our full-speed power consumption is about 375 watts and we have 2,400 Wh of stored energy in our 12-volt, 200-Ah battery bank.

Recharging this bank at a good rate of 50 amps will require a 600-watt charging source.

$$50 \text{ amps} \times 12 \text{ volts} = 600 \text{ watts}$$

A portable generator this size would appear to be capable of providing all the electrical power needed to supply the propulsion system, but most small generators are primarily AC, limiting DC output to around 10 amps. In any case, operating our boat directly from the generator is not only inefficient, it is contrary to the purpose of an electric craft. Therefore, our primary consideration for the use of a generator is battery replenishment.

Although the generator could just as easily be used while underway, the noise and fumes negate the purpose of the outing, so it is best used at stops or at camps. Extended outings in a craft of this type, where the capacity of the battery bank will be exceeded, usually involve overnight camping anyway, so a portable generator can serve dual functions.

Replenishing our 70-percent-depleted 200-Ah battery bank with a 10-amp source requires running the generator for more than 14 hours. If you can find one, the out-of-production Tanaka QEG-250 provides twice the output at half the weight—but no AC output.

Replacing the daily power consumption of our canoe in less than 8 hours requires a ratio of generator output to battery-bank capacity of about 1 to 10. If we apply this ratio to the 21,000-Wh bank in our sample 30-foot craft, it suggests a generator of about 2,000 watts. This unit most likely would be a four-cycle gasoline or diesel generator weighing between 60 and 130 pounds, not very significant for a 5,000-pound-displacement vessel. Appropriately installed, this small onboard generator could be a relatively inconspicuous piece of equipment, except when running, giving additional range (but not speed) to any outing.

In general, whether or not to use a generator to extend range comes back to intended use. When outing times do not exceed the capacity of the storage bank, a generator is impractical and unnecessary. If great range is required, an electrically propelled vessel might not be the appropriate craft. Where electric-boat characteristics are desired *and* extended range is a necessity, the generator certainly shines. The most common applications are for outings that include overnight stays in remote areas, where neither plugging in nor swapping batteries is possible.

Photovoltaics

Extending range with photovoltaics is limited at best, expensive for sure, and constantly at the mercy of old Sol. To look at what might be a practical application, let's develop the following model.

Our hull will have to be efficient, and therefore long and lean. Our power consumption will need to be equally lean and efficient. And we will need to carry ample reserve capacity to travel in low- or no-light hours.

Let's start with a 21-foot hull weighing 500 pounds completely stowed and manned. From the graph on page 79 we can see that this craft, powered by a 1-h.p. motor, will have an S/L ratio of 1.34, giving it a top speed of about 7 mph.

$$\text{Speed} = 1.34 \times \sqrt{(21)} = 6.14 \text{ knots or } 7.06 \text{ mph}$$

But the use of 1 h.p., or 750 watts, will not meet our "lean" power consumption criteria. Let's try 0.25 h.p. turning a large propeller through a reduction drive. This configuration may resemble a human-powered craft in its propulsion characteristics, and the amount of power expended is about the same. Using 0.25 h.p. to propel this vessel reduces the speed to a still-respectable 4 mph, and power consumption is reduced to 187.5 watts.

$$0.25 \text{ horsepower} \times 750 \text{ watts per horsepower} = 187.5 \text{ watts}$$

Our range for 8 hours (at 4 mph) is 32 miles. To meet our requirement of travel in low- or no-light conditions for 8 hours, we will need a reserve capacity of 1,500 Wh.

$$187.5 \text{ watts} \times 8 \text{ hours} = 1,500 \text{ watt-hours}$$

We can expect this capacity from a 125-Ah 12-volt battery.

$$1,500 \text{ watt-hours}/12 \text{ volts} = 125 \text{ amp-hours}$$

In ideal conditions photovoltaics can provide about 11 watts per square foot, and if we expect to see maybe 8 hours of sunshine, we will need about 17 square feet of collector area to supply our power requirements fully. Our estimates of insolation as well as output of the collector are both very generous here.

$$1,500 \text{ watt-hours}/(11 \text{ watts per square foot} \times 8 \text{ hours}) = 17.05 \text{ square feet}$$

We can see that our long, lean hull will be hard-pressed to carry a solar array this large. It would be more appropriate for a wider vessel or one with twin hulls.

At $6 per watt, our collector would cost $1,122, though after installation it would provide free, clean energy any time the sun was shining. The most effective use of photovoltaics requires proper orientation, cool temperatures, and, if possible, concentrating light directly on the collector.

Using photovoltaics to this extent to extend range in effect produces a solar-powered vessel. Assuming our boating is done in daylight hours, there is really no opportunity to recharge except during operation. Though this configuration might seem impractical at the current time, the use of photovoltaics does have practical merit in other battery-replenishment applications for electrically propelled craft.

PUTTING IT TOGETHER

The experimental solar-powered boat Clearwater *at the Minnsolar 92 solar-boat regatta.* Clearwater *is a 23-foot outrigger canoe running a stock Minn-Kota 3-h.p. submersible motor. (Photo courtesy Bud Roberts)*

The installation on the deck, canopy, or cabin roof of a few panels that produce 100 watts or more would go a long way toward keeping the battery bank of a large vessel topped off. When the boat isn't in use, a modest array could replenish the system entirely in just a few days. Of course, if a vessel with a 20,000-Wh bank is deeply discharged, a small rooftop array would require weeks to build a complete recharge; but since the battery is often only lightly discharged after a typical outing, it is conceivable that such a vessel could be operated only on weekends and never tap the grid.

If expense weren't a consideration, photovoltaics would be the most appropriate battery replenishment source for a stationary application. Using the roof of a

A 50-watt solar panel producing 3.02 amps at 16.9 volts. It measures 17.5 x 38.8 inches, weighs 13 pounds, and costs about $350. (Photo courtesy Bud Roberts)

boathouse, for example, a 100-square-foot array with optimum orientation could replenish a large battery bank of 20,000 watts every 3 days. This charging system would cost about $6,600 versus $2 for buying a charge from the grid, but it would provide independence from the line for a remote location. In most cases, after taking usage criteria and other recharging options into account, a considerably smaller array is just as adequate.

HYBRIDS

While on the subject of photovoltaics, generators, and extended range, it might be interesting to model a good hybrid craft. A vessel with the area necessary for an adequate PV array and the accommodations for extended outings of days or weeks may best be found in a houseboat or a barge. Speed does not play a critical role with these craft, and adequate displacement for ample reserves is easily accommodated. So ignoring expenses, let's design our model.

Many of the basic characteristics fall in line with the 30-foot vessel outlined previously except that this boat will be beamier and less efficient at the launch's speeds. Range can be about the same but at slower speeds.

To meet a 1:10 charge-to-capacity ratio, this boat's 20,000-Wh reserve capacity will require about 182 square feet of photovoltaics. This can easily fit atop the roof of a 30-foot vessel with an 8-foot beam and provide 2,000 watts per hour while the sun shines. This power alone can produce 2.67 h.p. from the 5-h.p. motor. We can also see from these numbers that operation at 5 h.p. will require about a day at low usage or inactivity to refurbish the system.

In the case of extended running or very poor solar conditions, a generator would be necessary. For this kind of boat, the generator could be in demand more often, and a unit rated at more than 2,000 watts might be desirable. However, the 2-kilowatt generator on our standard 30-foot vessel would be capable of running the boat at better than half-power under the poorest conditions—no sun and flat batteries. This hybrid vessel could have many creature comforts through its stored-energy potential. With an inverter to convert DC to AC, most necessary and unnecessary appliances commonplace in the home could be used afloat, without running the generator most of the time. And the large and heavy battery bank would lend substantial stability to this home-away-from-home platform.

SUMMARY

Designing appropriate electrical reserve capacity is mostly a matter of correctly estimating intended use. Extended range is best achieved by large electrical reserves or onboard generation from fossil fuel or photovoltaics. Charging stations within the range of a boat's reserve capacity will also allow longer distances to be traveled. Allowances must be made for the time required to recharge—overnight in most cases. With small boats, battery swaps can be the most practical method of extending range when not operating in a remote location.

Limits in the design of an electric boat are set by the hull's speed and its displacement. Working within these parameters, an infinite number of variations are possible.

CHAPTER 9

BUILDING A SIMPLE ELECTRIC BOAT

SOME YEARS BACK I BECAME INFATUATED with the idea of flying—not flying as in a commercial airliner, but building and flying an ultralight. A friend downriver had sparked this lofty idea by his own decision to build an airplane. When he obtained his plans and materials—mostly wood and foam held together with epoxy—I was immediately struck by their similarity to my boatbuilding materials. As the weeks passed and the parts approached a recognizable shape, I wondered if juniper could replace the aircraft-grade spruce and if the margin of error acceptable to a boatbuilder would be too great when building an airplane.

I borrowed a copy of the plans and found in the first paragraphs a statement that the world didn't need any more unfinished projects; if you undertake a project, finish it. Unlike me, my friend was more interested in flying aircraft than in building them, and after he got his pilot's license, the unfinished airplane was relegated to hanging from the rafters of his shop. Since my question about relative margins of error was never really answered, I decided to stick with building boats. I knew that, in the event something went wrong, I could swim much better than I could fly.

With this in mind, I hope to plant the idea of building a small, simple electric boat by providing the rough plans and a step-by-step narrative of the construction process. If the idea appeals to you, this project can be pulled off in about 60 or so hours—depending on the builder's constitution and skill. If it turns out well, there'll be many enjoyable boating hours ahead; if not, then you'll have an interesting conversation piece to adorn a corner of your shop.

A FIRST ELECTRIC BOAT

We can start by giving this boat a name. To remain gender-neutral, let's call it *Sam*, which can be short for *Samuel* or *Samantha*. *Sam* is about 14 feet 6 inches in length overall with a beam of about 30 inches. *Sam* can carry up to 300 pounds and weigh as little as 85 pounds without the battery, depending on the kinds of wood used and the thickness of the boards. Designed around the needs of one person, *Sam* is much like the Black River Guide mentioned in Chapter 1. Steering is set up for the left hand, with speed control for the right. I find this setup best for a right-handed person, but it can be changed if you prefer a different arrangement.

Sam is an open boat, and to some may be a bit tender, but it rides low in the water and has a shallow draft, good for small lakes or streams with few wakes and strong currents. Its simplicity makes it easy to handle and easy to keep clean. It could best be considered an electric canoe.

There is one thing to bear in mind if you decide to take on this project: keep it simple. This doesn't mean taking shortcuts or doing shoddy work, nor does it imply that the completed boat will be an ugly duckling. The true beauty of *Sam* is its simplicity.

Sam's birthing will be laid out in four steps, explained in detail later. Each step requires different tools, different materials, and the use of different areas of the brain. If you approach the project in this manner, you're less apt to get burned out on boatbuilding.

FOUR STEPS

Step 1: Purchasing materials. This is the most important of the four steps as it requires the commitment of financial resources. Having all the materials on hand at the start is important for two reasons. First, the commitment of money to the project will make it real, not just a pipe dream. Second, it will be very important to see, touch, measure, and experience all the components at the onset so the mind can visualize how they fit together.

Everyone has his or her own favorite brands or products. Substituting these is fine as long as they meet the physical requirements. I recommend specific brands in the materials list because I know how they work and what to expect. If you have your own choice that does the same thing, then use it.

All the components to build this simple boat are available to most anyone, anywhere, off the shelf of the local hardware store, lumberyard, or discount store.

Step 2: Constructing the wooden components. The hull, the largest and most important component, is built from just seven pieces of wood. But don't let a completed hull lull you into thinking you're almost finished: The majority of the painstaking or thoughtful work comes in the smaller parts that set *Sam* apart as an electric boat.

For Step 2 you'll need a place to work that is dry and, if it's a cold time of the year, heated: Epoxy cures all too slowly in a cold shop. And you'll need to complete the woodwork before moving on to the next step: Wood dust is detrimental to the application of a good finish, and neither metal shavings nor oil is good to have around bare wood.

Step 3: *Preparing the motor and fabricating the control parts.* In some ways this step will be like working in the dark since progress will be more difficult to measure than it was for the hull, which by now occupies floor space. Approach each piece of work with its intended function in mind. When appropriate, fit pieces together to see how they work and if they fit too loosely or snugly.

The control parts are the components that will see the most action. They are simple, but they must be sufficiently rugged to withstand abuse. A failure could leave you in a very awkward position on the water, usually at the worst of times. Because these parts are small and often require metalwork (although a few are wooden) they can be built away from the hull-construction site, perhaps in a shop equipped with metalworking tools.

Step 4: *Assembling and finishing.* Assembly requires wiring and some adjustments to the control parts made earlier. Most of the finish work will be sanding—the drudge work of any shop. *Sam* is a good-looking boat and should not be short-changed with a hastily applied finish. A finish is only as good as the preparation that goes into it; don't devalue the hours spent building the boat with inadequate attention to detail. A quality finish will last many years and make *Sam* easy to clean, but more important, it will promote respect for the little craft, enjoyment of its use, and pride in ownership.

TOOLS

In addition to the desire to build a boat and a place to build it, you'll need certain skills and tools. For anyone the least bit handy, the skills should be no problem. If you're one of those lucky persons who don't know the difference between a screwdriver and a corkscrew, maybe this project isn't for you. You might find it easier and more satisfying to purchase a ready-made electric boat.

Following is a list of tools and their degrees of importance. If you don't have these tools, you'll need to get them. And if you don't know how to use them properly, learn *before* you jump into this project.

Essential Power Tools

- A bandsaw. It need not be a large or powerful saw, but it should be equipped with a sharp, ⅜-inch-wide blade. A high-quality sabersaw—like a Bosch—can be substituted if you're prepared to pay the price in time and misery. A sabersaw is required in one operation in the construction.
- A router. Used mostly for corner rounds using ⅜- and ¼-inch-radius bits.
- A table saw or a radial-arm saw. Desirable but perhaps the least essential. Substituting a hand-held Skilsaw is possible if you're highly skilled.
- An electric drill. Necessary for fabricating metal parts as well as drilling into wood. The drill should be powerful and supplied with ⅛-, ³⁄₁₆-, ¼-, and ⁵⁄₁₆-inch metal-cutting bits, 1¼-, 1⅛-, 1-, ⁷⁄₁₆-, and ½-inch bits for wood and a Phillips bit for driving screws. Spade bits for the large sizes are fine.
- A belt sander. This tool will see a lot of use. Have extra fresh belts on hand in grits 50, 80, and 120.

Good-to-Have Tools

- A Skilsaw. Essential if you don't have a table saw.
- A sabersaw. Essential if you don't have a bandsaw.
- A jointer.
- A palm sander.
- A thickness planer.

Essential Hand Tools

- A hacksaw. Fit it with a new blade for mild steel and have another blade to back it up.
- Bar clamps. Four or more bar clamps or pipe clamps with a 30-inch span—the more, the better.
- C-clamps. At least four.
- Screwdrivers. Both Phillips and slot-head screwdrivers in various sizes.
- A set punch.
- A file.
- A sanding block. Buy a rubber one or cut one from a scrap of wood.
- Crimping pliers. For electrical connections.
- Wire cutters with a stripper.
- A tubing cutter for stock up to 1¼ inches.
- A clamping work table (WorkMate or similar).
- A hand plane.
- A soldering iron or torch and electrical-grade solder and flux.
- A varnish-quality paintbrush.
- Disposable gloves.

Most of these tools are a part of the average home shop. The more of them you already have, the easier the work, as you know where they are as well as how to use them. Most of the work in the project ahead is close handwork and involves little heavy machinery except the bandsaw.

DRAWINGS

On the theory that a picture is worth a thousand words, I have included sketches of all the components for *Sam's* construction. They are followed by some assembly drawings, which I hope will clarify the process when my words fail to do so. Familiarity with these drawings will make the rest of this chapter easier to follow. These drawings are for illustrative purposes only and are not to scale.

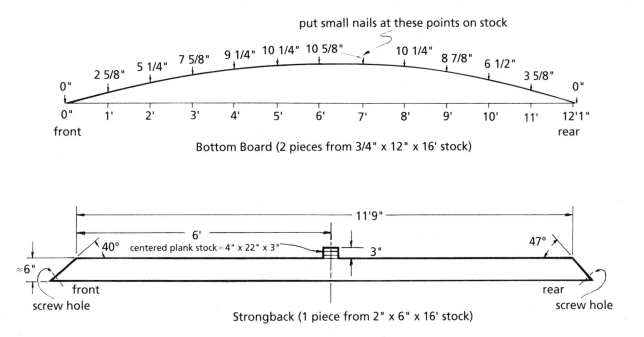

Sheet 1
Not to scale.

92

Sheet 2
Not to scale.

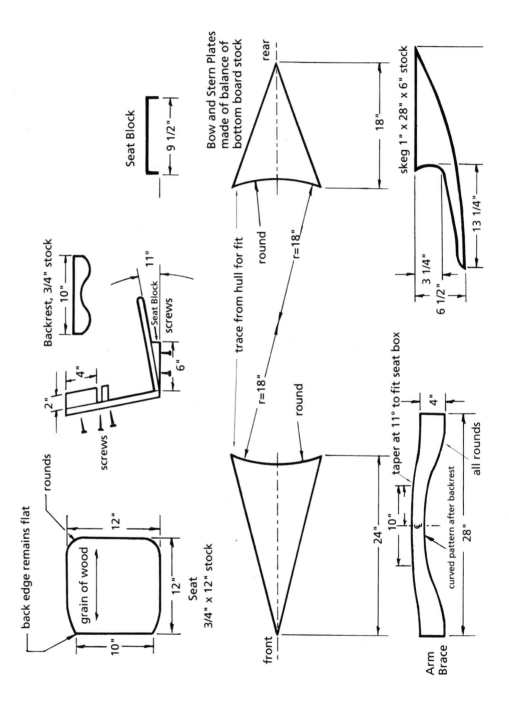

Seat Block

9 1/2"

Bow and Stern Plates
made of balance of
bottom board stock

rear

round

r=18"

trace from hull for fit

r=18"

round

18"

skeg 1" x 28" x 6" stock

13 1/4"

3 1/4"

6 1/2"

Backrest, 3/4" stock

10"

11°

Seat Block

screws

2"

4"

screws

6"

front

24"

10"

taper at 11° to fit seat box

4"

curved pattern after backrest

all rounds

28"

Arm
Brace

back edge remains flat

rounds

grain of wood

12"

12"

10"

Seat
3/4" x 12" stock

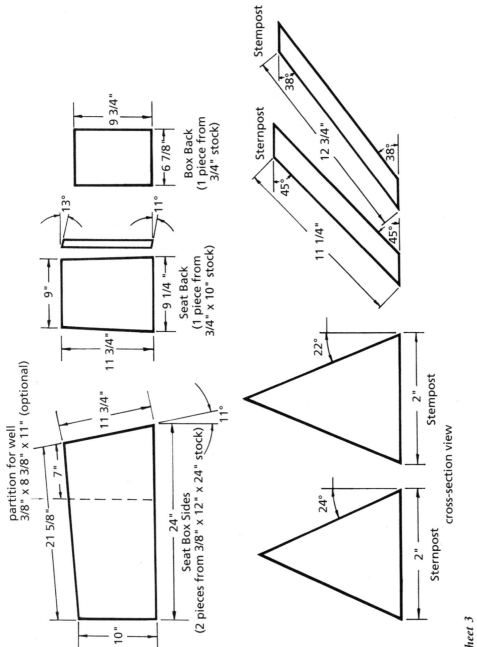

9 3/4"

6 7/8"

Box Back
(1 piece from
3/4" stock)

13°   11°

9"   9 1/4"

11 3/4"

Seat Back
(1 piece from
3/4" x 10" stock)

partition for well
3/8" x 8 3/8" x 11" (optional)

11 3/4"   11°

7"

21 5/8"   24"

10"

Seat Box Sides
(2 pieces from 3/8" x 12" x 24" stock)

Stempost

38°

12 3/4"

38°

Sternpost

45°

45°

11 1/4"

22°

2"

Stempost

24°

2"

Sternpost

cross-section view

Sheet 3
Not to scale.

94

Sheet 4. Metal Control Parts
Not to scale.

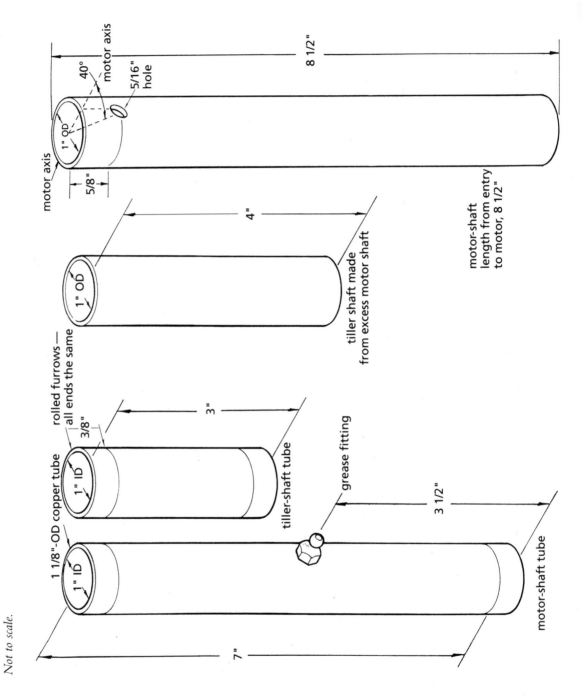

motor axis

40°

motor axis

5/16" hole

1" OD

motor axis

5/8"

8 1/2"

motor-shaft length from entry to motor, 8 1/2"

1" OD

4"

tiller shaft made from excess motor shaft

rolled furrows — all ends the same

3/8"

1" ID

3"

tiller-shaft tube

1 1/8"-OD copper tube

grease fitting

1" ID

3 1/2"

7"

motor-shaft tube

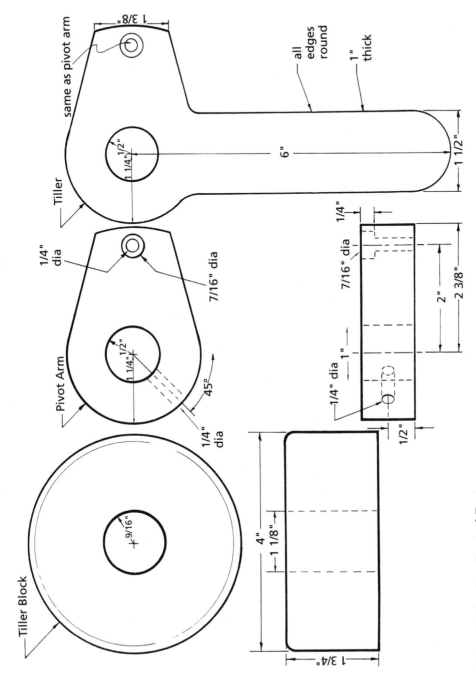

Sheet 5. Wooden Control Parts
Not to scale.

Sheet 6
Not to scale.

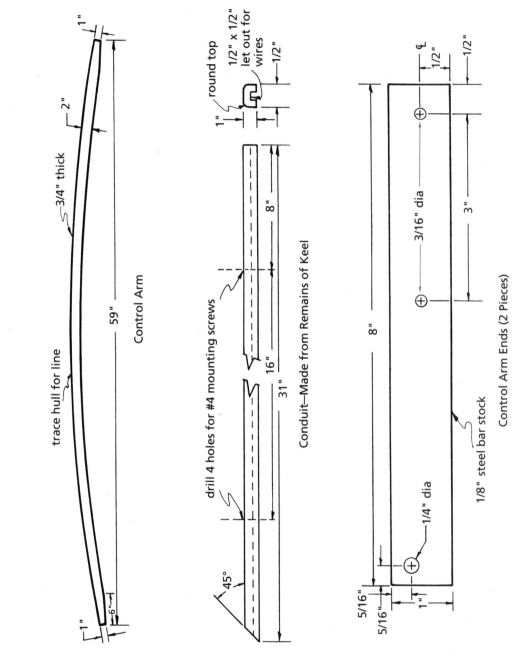

1"

2"

3/4" thick

59"

trace hull for line

6"

1"

Control Arm

round top

1/2" x 1/2"
let out for
wires

1"

1/2"

drill 4 holes for #4 mounting screws

8"

16"

31"

45°

Conduit—Made from Remains of Keel

℄

1/2"

1/2"

3/16" dia

3"

8"

1/8" steel bar stock

1/4" dia

5/16"

5/16"

1"

Control Arm Ends (2 Pieces)

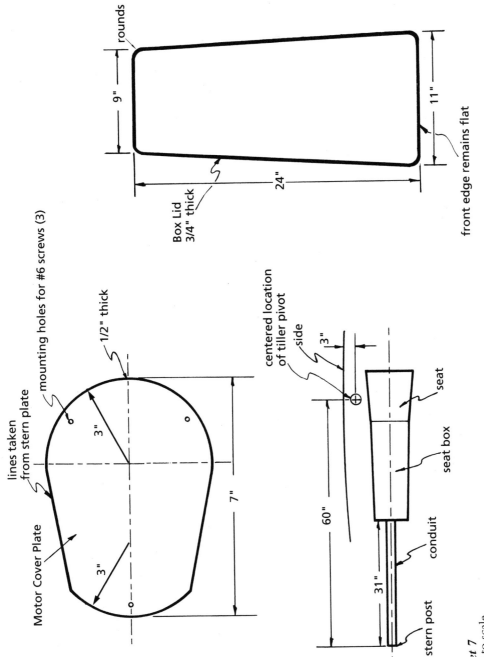

rounds

9"

11"

24"

front edge remains flat

Box Lid
3/4" thick

mounting holes for #6 screws (3)

1/2" thick

lines taken
from stern plate

Motor Cover Plate

3"

3"

7"

centered location
of tiller pivot

side

3"

seat

seat box

60"

31"

conduit

stern post

Sheet 7
Not to scale.

*Assembly of Motor
Shaft to Control
Arm*

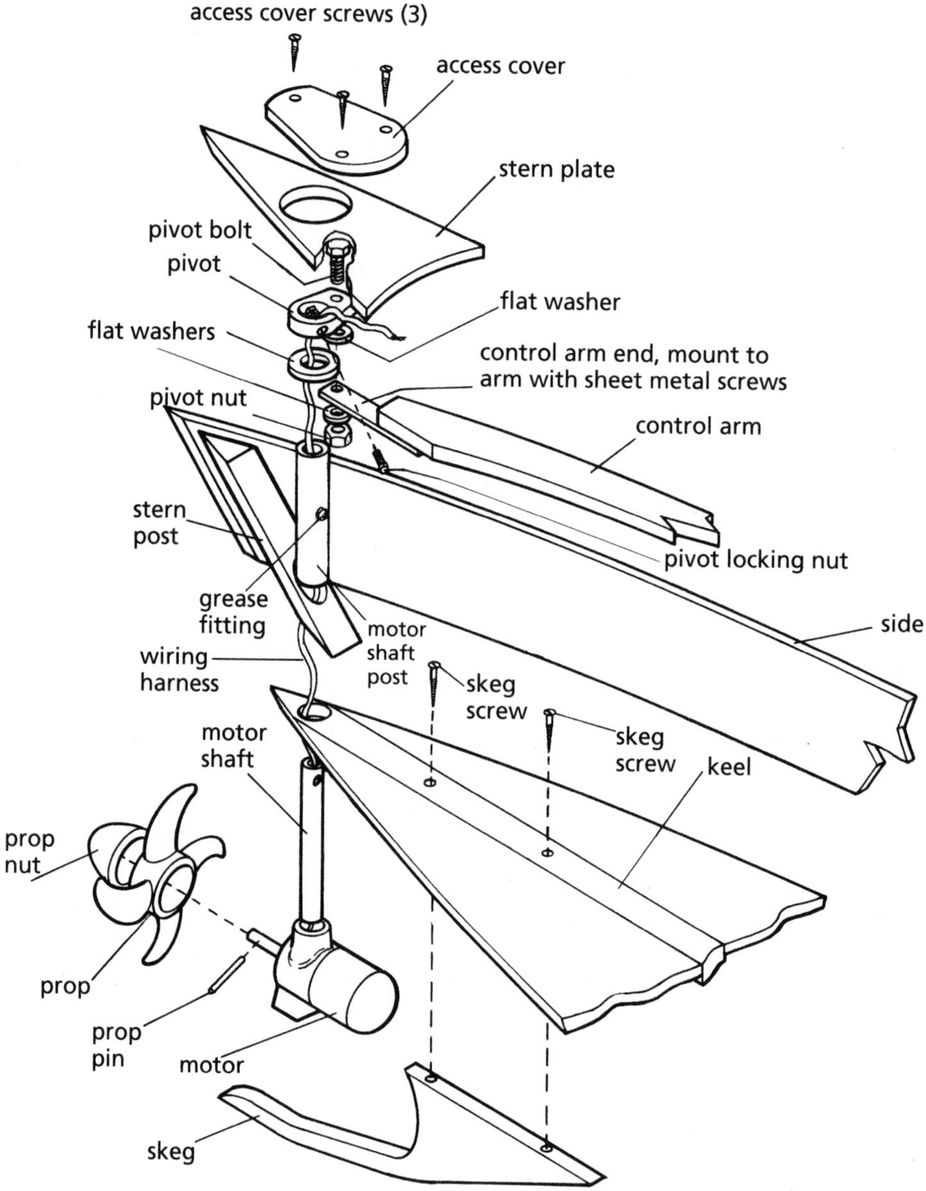

access cover screws (3)

access cover

stern plate

pivot bolt

pivot

flat washer

flat washers

control arm end, mount to
arm with sheet metal screws

pivot nut

control arm

stern
post

pivot locking nut

grease
fitting

motor
shaft
post

wiring
harness

skeg
screw

side

motor
shaft

skeg
screw

keel

prop
nut

prop

prop
pin

motor

skeg

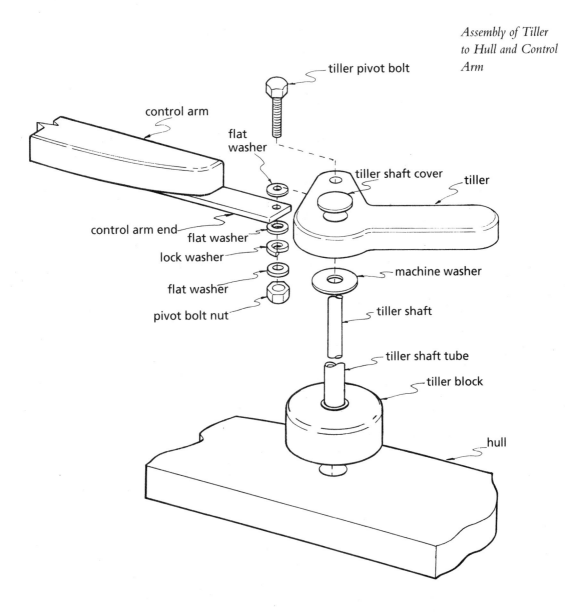

tiller pivot bolt

control arm

flat washer

tiller shaft cover

tiller

control arm end

flat washer

lock washer

flat washer

pivot bolt nut

machine washer

tiller shaft

tiller shaft tube

tiller block

hull

Assembly of Seat
Box and Seat

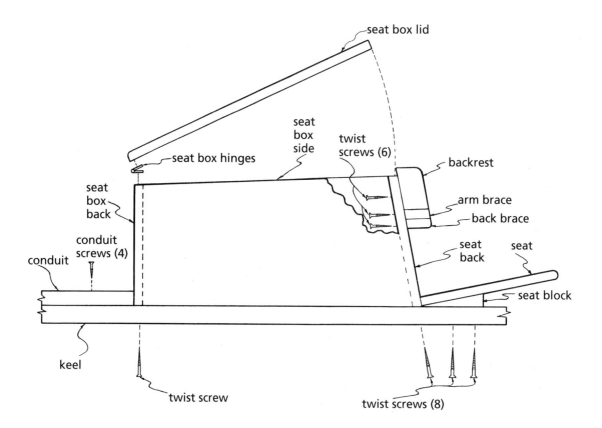

STEP 1: PURCHASING MATERIALS

Following is a list of the materials required to complete *Sam,* namely, wood, hardware, and chemicals.

Wood

Sam is a wooden boat. The wood of choice for the hull is Atlantic white cedar. Other cedars can be substituted, depending on regional availability. The advantage of cedar is its light weight; that cedar is also rot resistant is not so much a factor since the entire boat will be sealed in epoxy. This wood may be the most difficult to obtain off the shelf of the local lumberyard.

Don't settle for inferior material. The wood should be clear if possible, tight-knotted if not. Avoid planks with the water vein or with large knots. And if you don't have the tools necessary to produce material of the specified dimensions, take the lumber to a mill shop and have them do the required work.

For the keel and rubrails, my choice of woods is black walnut, but much latitude exists here. The objective is to use hardwood. The contrasting color of walnut or mahogany is attractive but not essential. Oak or ash could be used. Obtaining 16-foot-long boards is not necessary; shorter pieces may be spliced to make up the required length.

Pecan is the wood of choice for control parts, but you can use oak as well. This wood must be a full inch thick after dressing, and you might find just what you need in the scrap box of a good cabinet shop.

Cedar
- Two 12" × ¾" × 16' (bottom boards)
- Two 10" × ⅝" × 16' (sides)
- One 12" × ¾" × 6' (seat and box)
- One 12" × ⅜" × 6' (box)

Walnut
- Two 1" × ½" × 16' (rails)
- One 1½" × 1" × 16' (keel)
- One 7" x 1" × 48" (skeg)
- One 6" x ¾" × 36" (seat brace and tiller)

Other
- One 2" × 6" × 16' (strongback—pine)
- One 1" × 5" × 12" (control part—pecan)
- One 2" × 4" × 6' (posts, seat, miscellaneous—fir)
- One 3' × ⁷⁄₁₆" dowel (caps for screws)

(Note: 2" × 6" for the strongback is a nominal dimension, but for all other components you will need the actual dimensions listed; i.e., bottom boards need to be a full 12 inches wide.)

Hardware

The motor. The most important piece of hardware is the motor. You will take it from an electric outboard—a trolling motor—which is most easily and economically obtained from a discount store. As you will be using only the lower unit, propeller, and the switches, a transom mount is more than satisfactory; you don't need a motor equipped with a bow mount or a foot control. You might be able to find a good value on a cosmetically damaged or a reconditioned unit.

When it comes to power, bigger is not always better. A motor producing from 24 to 36 pounds of thrust is satisfactory. A smaller motor may yield lower top speed but is much more efficient in that it limits the power consumption when run flat-out. The difference between a 24- and a 36-pound-thrust motor is less than 0.5 mph at top speed.

The most important specifications of the trolling motor are a 1-inch shaft diameter and built-in reverse. Usually the speed control includes five forward speeds and two in reverse, which simplifies wiring and eliminates the purchase of additional switches. Using a variable speed control is not out of the question—if you're electrically inclined.

The size and pitch of the propeller are also important. A large prop greatly increases draft, and though the larger prop has definite performance advantages, a smaller propeller will prove satisfactory.

Some of the available trolling motors with these characteristics are MotorGuide, Zebco, old Pfluegers, Shakespeare, and probably others. Unfortunately the Minn-Kota does not have a 1-inch shaft and is equipped with a rather large prop, but if you're willing to face these problems to use this unit, the end result will prove satisfactory. I recommend the 25-pound-thrust MotorGuide using a small four-blade prop. This unit features five forward speeds and two in reverse, and costs about $130.

The battery. Most of the other hardware for *Sam* is easily and inexpensively obtained at most any hardware store. The one exception is the battery, which represents a large investment. Select a DCM or EV battery rated at 105 Ah or higher. The most common and economical configuration is a 115-Ah DCM battery with outside dimensions of about 13 inches × 6⅞ inches × 9 inches high. A good price is about $75. Remember that the battery must fit in a battery box, so don't get one too large. An open-cell battery is less expensive, but a sealed battery is also an option.

To keep your battery "hot," you need some kind of charger. An inexpensive battery charger with a 10-amp rating is OK. Larger units with automatic features are, of course, better.

- One 25-pound-thrust trolling motor
- One 115-Ah EV or DCM battery
- One 10-amp battery charger
- One roll of electrical tape
- Fasteners
- One hundred 1⅝" #6 drywall screws
- Twenty-five 2" #6 drywall screws
- One 2½" #8 brass Phillips–head wood screw (skeg)
- One 2" #8 brass Phillips–head wood screw (skeg)
- Three 1" #6 brass Phillips–head wood screws (cover)
- Four 1½" #4 brass Phillips–head wood screws (conduit)
- Two 1½" × ¼" machine screws (pivots)
- One 1¼" × ¼" machine screw (motor shaft)
- Eight ¼" flat washers
- Eight ¼" lock washers
- Three ¼" locking nuts
- Four ¾" #6 sheet-metal screws (control arm)

Other hardware

- One 12" × 1"-ID hard-copper plumbing pipe
- One ¼" straight grease fitting
- One brass nut to fit grease fitting threads
- One 1"-ID machine washer
- One pair of 2½" × ¾" brass hinges with screws
- Two 1" × 8" × ⅛" flat-rolled steel bar stock

Chemicals

Epoxy. Much of the difference between building a boat now and 100 years ago is related to the chemicals available today. Epoxies are the greatest thing since grits. Working with them is easy once you have a basic understanding of how they behave. Two types of epoxy are used in the construction of *Sam*; one functions as a glue and the other as a sealant. Many different epoxy manufacturers vie for the business of boatbuilders. As a small-time user we must choose from those brands readily available in small quantities. I recommend Evercoat's epoxy glue for gluing, and Gluvit as a sealant. Other brands may work just as well, so if you are familiar with the properties of a different brand, by all means use it. Regardless of the brand, epoxies and their solvents produce hazardous vapors and are dangerous to bare skin. Treat them with the respect they warrant and read the precautions on the labels.

Curing times for the epoxies used in this project are affected by temperature. In an 80°F shop, epoxy glue should set in 4 to 6 hours and allow at least 30 minutes of working time. The thinner epoxy sealant will not set as fast, which is good because you will need the additional time to work it into the wood.

Varnish. *Sam* is finished with varnish—marine varnish to be exact. Pigmented paints can be used but aren't recommended. As with epoxies, there are many brands of marine varnish from which to chose. The one important feature to look for is a high UV-filter content. A good varnish is expensive but repays the expense in the quality of the finish and the ease of application. I recommend Z-Spar's Captain's Varnish.

Here's what to buy:

- 1 pint of epoxy glue
- 1 quart of Gluvit
- 1 gallon of lacquer thinner
- 1 quart of Captain's Varnish

These materials, assembled in the correct fashion, will produce *Sam*. The cost will depend on the deal you get on the big-ticket items such as the battery and the trolling motor. The total cost may be about $500.

Shop around and get to know what is available, how it performs, and what it costs. Some suppliers can be of great help when you are selecting materials. Unfortunately, most of them never see the product in use, and they are primarily interested in making a sale. Beware. If you chance to visit a builder's shop, don't aggravate him or her with a bunch of thoughtless questions. Look about to see which tools get the greatest use. See which chemicals are used. Be informed enough to ask intelligent questions.

Now that you have committed to the project by dropping the bucks, let's move on.

STEP 2: CONSTRUCTING THE WOODEN COMPONENTS

The first thing we must do—after putting the chemicals safely out of the reach of children and pets, and the wood away so it will remain dry—is to construct a strongback. This support holds the boat in position during the construction of the hull; after that it is of no value—except maybe to build another boat. If you have a WorkMate or equivalent clamping table, now is the time to put it to excellent use to hold the strongback; later it can also serve as a rest for the boat. If you don't have a WorkMate, then fashion legs for the strongback—much like a sawhorse.

A well-used strongback mounted in a clamping table. This one has an extension for building different-size boats.

The Hull

Mark one of the 16-foot bottom boards for cutting by partially driving small nails at the locations indicated on sheet 1 (page 91). Bend a flexible strip of wood, such as one of the rail pieces, against the nails in a fair, smooth curve from stem to stern. Start the curve at one end of the board as the remaining wood will be used later.

Cut this bottom board along the curve at 90 degrees to the plane of the board. You will almost certainly need help holding the work when cutting. After you cut one board, use it as a template to mark the second one. You can cut both boards at the same time if you tack them together (in a waste area) so they won't slip, but they will be more difficult to handle this way.

Lay the two cut bottom boards aside and identify the lumber for the keel. Using the router and a ¼-inch corner-round bit, round both sides of the *bottom* of the keel the length of the piece. The keel is 1½ inches wide and 1 inch deep; be careful not to round the wrong sides. Cut the keel, making it longer than the bottom boards by 8 inches. The remaining piece of material will be used later, so make sure to leave at least 31 inches of excess. Dry-fit the bottom boards against the keel to check their alignment and, with the keel extending by 4 inches at both ends, draw a pencil line or two across the fitted work for indexing later. If the bottom boards buck after being cut, that is, take on a curve due to the alteration to the tensions in the boards, it may be necessary to straighten the edges. Do this with a chalkline and a jointer or hand plane.

BUILDING A SIMPLE ELECTRIC BOAT

The boat bottom consists of the two bottom halves glued to the keel. Viewed bottom-down and sanded; the two pieces are the stem and sternpost.

Mount other planks temporarily across the strongback to make a support table, and glue the bottom boards to the keel. Make sure the bow and stern of the bottom boards are identified and properly aligned. Use enough epoxy to squeeze out all along both sides of the joints. Be sure the epoxy is thick enough to stay in place and to bridge any gaps in the fit. The bottom boards should be flush with the keel on what is to be the inside of the boat, which at this time should be up. It's not easy to get everything lined up quickly, but the epoxy allows enough time, so take what you need to ensure all is right.

Drywall screws installed in drilled pilot holes may be used at the ends of the bottom boards to hold them in place. Clamps are used elsewhere; you need at least four. Remember that with an epoxy joint, a little squeeze is all that's necessary; avoid high clamping pressure. Check with a straight-edge to see that the plane of the bottom is flat; stagger the clamps to prevent bowing. Drag a gloved finger through the squeeze-out on the bottom side to form a neat fillet between the bottom boards and the keel. Set this assembly aside to cure.

Use the table saw to cut the stem and sternpost from your piece of 2 × 4 fir. Mount them to the ends of the strongback, screwed from the bottom of the strongback.

When the bottom assembly is fully cured, sand the inside with the belt sander to smooth away excess epoxy and level the boards to the keel. Start with 80-grit and work through to 120. You will not have an opportunity to fully sand this piece again, so do it all now. If this is your first time using a belt sander, take note: You can do more damage in 30 seconds than you can repair in an hour if you're not careful. Practice on some scrap if you're not experienced with this machine.

Align the bottom assembly to the strongback and the stem and sternpost. Mark and drill four pilot holes to hold the bottom to the strongback and the posts. Some excess of bottom boards and keel should overlap the posts. Pencil an extension of the

The untrimmed bottom ready to be fastened to the sternpost and screwed to the strongback for temporary support.

edges of the bottom pieces to intersect on the keel; be sure you place the screws in the posts at least an inch back from this intersection so they won't be in the way when trimming the bottom. Fit up dry, index with pencil lines, and glue the bottom assembly to the posts only. The plank stack in the center of the strongback will introduce about 3 inches of curvature—*rocker*—into the bottom.

For this particular operation, very little glue is required. Apply the glue to one side of the joint with a small stick or a gloved finger, taking care not to put any where it doesn't belong—on the strongback, in this case. This is an excellent application for "freezer glue." Leftover epoxy glue, if placed in a freezer immediately, may be kept for several days. Since all components are screwed in place, work may continue.

Start by removing the four screws at the ends of the bottom boards that you previously installed to hold them to the keel. Now you are going to recut the perimeter of the bottom to give it a 21-degree angle from the perpendicular. Scribing a line around the perimeter of the bottom about ¼ inch from the edge will help guide your saw. The idea is to bevel the perimeter in the same plane as the two posts. This makes the top surface (outside) of the bottom smaller than the bottom surface (inside), which should remain at its original dimension. Using a circular saw or sabersaw, rough-trim the bottom to this angle, then smooth it with a belt sander to a flowing line flush with the posts. If you make a slight error on the bevel, it can be filled later, but keep the curve regular so the inside of the boat shows a good fit.

For this next operation you'll need a helper. Find the balance point of one of the side boards and mark it, then lay the board in place, allowing the extra length to

The bottom fastened to the sternpost with trimming underway. Note that the screw to the post is not in the way of trimming.

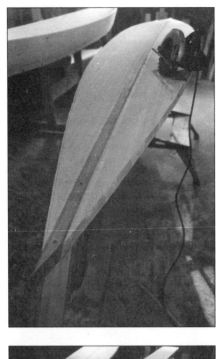

The side board in the process of being glued and screwed in place.

run off evenly at both ends. Drill pilot holes at the balance-point mark and at 2-foot intervals along the side board. Drill the holes at a 21-degree angle (or close). When you're sure of the fit, apply glue to one edge of the bottom and that side of the posts, fit up the side board, and screw it in place. Try to hold the amount of side board that extends above the work surface to ¼ inch or less, but don't be greatly concerned; this will all be trimmed later. Anywhere gaps appear, add extra screws. Also, screw the side board to the posts with as many screws as necessary for a gap-free joint. The screws can be removed later, or they can be run in and patched over. It makes little difference mechanically, but aesthetically, patched-over screws look worse. If you plan to remove the screws, use a ¼-inch washer under the heads to prevent crushing the wood.

As the work is screwed in place, you may continue work on the other side, but first you need to trim the excess from the ends of the mounted side board and belt-sand them flush with the exposed side of the posts. It is easy to mess up this cut, so take care to make it correctly, using a straightedge and visual alignment. With the stem and stern of the first side board trimmed and flush, fit and glue the other side following the same procedure. You must stop now and let all parts cure. Go to work on the seat box if you wish.

After the hull cures, remove all screws (leave the screws that hold the keel to

The side boards in place, ready to be trimmed. Screws have washers at their necks to prevent crushing the wood.

the strongback for now) or run them in for patching. All screws must be removed from the sternpost. Use a hand plane to remove the excess of the side boards, and sand them flush with the bottom. Dress the bow and stern accordingly. Use a glue and sanding-dust mixture to patch all screw holes, gaps, and defects. Remove the four screws you installed to hold the bottom to the strongback and to the posts,

Left: *Shaving the excess from the bottom of the side boards. This can be delayed until the last step before assembly if desired.*
Right: *The empty hull rightside up. The inside will require little sanding but the outside remains to be dressed. Disregard the over-length stem and sternpost. Drawing dimensions should result in posts about 1 inch shorter than the hull sides.*

BUILDING A SIMPLE ELECTRIC BOAT

and lift off the hull. Remove the strongback from the shop—its work is done—and place the hull on the top of the work table, rightside up.

The Seat and Box

Much of this work can be done while waiting for the hull's glue joints to cure. The seat and box are the beginnings of what sets *Sam* apart from other small boats. This is where you're always going to be while on the water, so you want to make them comfortable and strong.

Cut out the seat back, the box sides, and the box back. Assemble these into a box using glue and finish nails, setting and patching the nails. The components are butt-jointed, with the sides over the back and seat back. Be sure the box is *plumb* (equal corner-to-corner diagonal measurements) before setting it aside to cure.

Cut out the seat, seat block, back brace, backrest, and lid. Use the router and a ⅜-inch corner-round bit to round all (top and bottom) but the back edge of the seat and all (top and bottom) but the front edge of the lid (see sheets 2 and 3, pages 92 and 93). Mount the seat block to the bottom of the seat using glue and screws. Cut out the arm brace and round all the edges except where the brace intersects the seat box, the backrest, and the hull.

After the box has cured, sand all sides flush.

Moving to the hull, measure from the intersection of the sternpost with the keel 31 inches toward the bow. This is the correct location for the back of the seat box.

Two hulls with seats and boxes installed. The object in the front of the near boat is a weight for counterbalance. Again, disregard pictured post lengths.

Centering it side to side, dry-fit the seat box to the hull. Some material might have to be removed from the base of the box to attain a good fit. Once the box is properly positioned, outline it, then remove it and drill four pilot holes through the bottom, two each for screws into the box back and seat back. Glue and screw the box in place. Mount the seat in front of the box, following the same procedure.

The arm brace is a major structural component and should be fitted with care. It serves as the primary handling point, prevents the sides from flexing, and helps reinforce the bottom of the boat. This three-point connection—both sides, bottom, and seat back—stiffens the hull significantly. Dry-fit the arm brace in place, along with the back brace and the backrest. Make sure all the mounting screws are well seated and that there is a good fit between the ends of the arm brace and the hull. When you are sure that the fit is good and that all exposed edges have been rounded, glue and screw the back brace, arm brace, and the backrest in place. None of the screws used in the seat box/arm brace assembly should be removed. The screws through the bottom of the boat should be run in and patched. Seat those through the side flush; they will be covered by the rail. The screws through the seat back are seated flush from inside the box.

The bow and stern plates are made from the remains of a bottom board. Using a jointer is the easiest way to put the proper angle on the sides for an easy fit into the hull, but a table saw can be used if it is set up properly. The bow plate should be almost a straight fit, but the stern plate may require some additional fitting. Round the open end of both pieces—top and bottom— then dry-fit them to the hull. Glue and screw them in place. The screws will be covered by the rail and need only be seated flush. Drill a 7/16-inch hole in the bow plate clear of the stempost, or about 8 inches from the tip of the boat; this is for the bow line.

Measure back along both sides 3 inches from the tip of the stem and from the stern, and mark these four locations on the hull. Holding the rails to the side of the boat— you might need a helper again— transfer these marks to the rail; these are the locations for screws

Hull with stem and stern plates, seat, box, arm brace, and backrest mounted. The plates in this photo are walnut, and the arm brace is somewhat different from Sam's.

Check the complete hull for pilot marks and other areas that need special attention.

holding the rail ends to the hull. Use a ⁷⁄₁₆-inch wood bit to drill a shallow hole (for a plug) on the outside surface of the rails at these marked locations, centered top to bottom. Follow this with a pilot hole through the rail in the center of each of the plug holes. Dry-fit one rail and trim the ends to allow the other rail to be mounted. Remove, apply the glue, and install the rail, starting at one end and using short finish nails sparsely to hold it flush with the top of the side. Use clamps whenever possible, or exclusively if you want to avoid nail holes. Always nail from the outside in through the rail. Set the nails (if not too long) or pull them out; you can patch the holes later. When both rails are glued in place, cut four plugs from the ⁷⁄₁₆-inch dowel and cap the screws. Using your gloved finger, pull a fillet on the epoxy squeeze-out at the bottom of the rail. Set this aside to cure.

After all the components of the hull are cured, sand the rails flush to the top of the side boards. Sand the plugs flush. Sand the excess epoxy from the bow and stern plates, and use a ⅜-inch corner-round bit in the router to round all the working surfaces—the top edge of the rail, the top inside of the hull, and all intersections with the bow and stern plates and the arm brace. Be careful at the tips of the stem and stern; these areas are best worked by hand.

The hull is now basically complete and should look pretty much like a boat. The underside and the side patches will be worked down later. For now, set the boat aside and get ready to make control parts and take a look at the motor.

STEP 3: PREPARING THE MOTOR
AND FABRICATING THE CONTROL PARTS

For this stage of the construction, you will be working with metal. Separate this work from the wooden parts of the boat. For a while the electric drill and a good set-punch are the tools of choice. Your first project is to disassemble the trolling motor.

The Motor

The only components of the trolling motor we are interested in are the lower unit, or the motor itself, the propeller and its fastener, and the wiring, including the battery clamps and the switches. What you are about to do will void any warranty on the unit, so now is the time to make sure it's OK. Before proceeding further, mount the intact trolling motor and connect it to a battery, first making sure all switches are in the Off position. Operating the unit out of water is not a good practice but permissible for evaluation. Try all speed settings and reverse, operating the unit for only the time necessary to determine if the unit is sound—no more than a few minutes. If all is well, proceed as follows.

First remove the propeller, then open the head and disconnect all the wires, labeling each one so you can reconnect them to the proper tabs. Remove the switches. Finally, remove the head from the motor shaft. When you are finished, you should have the lower unit with its shaft, the propeller and its fastener, and the main switch and the leads that go to the battery. Some units have a secondary switch and relay; put these aside, along with the transom mount and the remains of the head. *Do not under any circumstances disassemble the lower unit.*

With a tubing cutter, cut the motor shaft 8½ inches above the point where it enters the motor housing. You only get one chance at this cut, so make sure of your measurement, and take care not to cut the wires running inside the tube. From the cut-off portion of the motor shaft, cut off a 4-inch piece, measuring for this piece from the previous cut. This will be the tiller shaft. Lay aside the remains of the motor shaft to be used later for alignment purposes. Stuff a small rag, which must be removed later, down the motor shaft still attached to the lower unit to prevent metal shavings from falling into the motor housing. With a file, dress a bevel on the outside ends of the freshly cut tubing to remove the lip left by the cutter; leave the inside of the tube alone.

Cut two pieces from the 1-inch-ID hard-copper tubing, one 7 inches long and the other 3 inches long. Dress the ends inside and out so they fit over the motor shaft easily. You can use the remains of the motor shaft for fitting purposes. About ⅜ inch from each end of the two pieces of tubing, roll a furrow into the

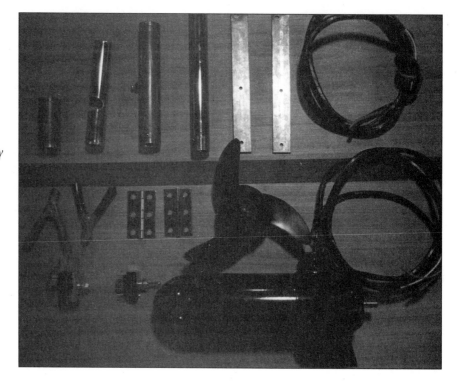

The metal control parts and hardware. Shown are motor, prop, control-arm ends, motor tube and shaft, tiller tube and shaft (differing slightly from Sam's), battery clamps, hinges, and switches. The extra wiring harness and switch shown are not necessary for Sam. Also, it is neither necessary nor advisable to remove the motor shaft from the motor housing.

copper with the tubing cutter, checking this with the motor shaft until a snug fit is achieved. Do not make a deep cut. It might be best to try this first on the remnant of the copper pipe to get a feel for how to achieve the desired effect.

The larger of the two copper pieces is the motor-shaft tube. Shape one surface of the brass nut that fits the threads of your grease fitting to the curvature of the tubing and solder it on the center of this tube. Because you are soldering copper, you can use electrical solder.

For a good solder joint, the mating surfaces must be clean. To get a clean surface, use fine sandpaper, first marking the fitting location with a punch. With a soldering iron or a torch with a soldering tip, heat the clean copper tubing until it is warm to the touch, then brush flux onto the solder area. Continue heating the tubing until it is hot enough to melt solder touched to its surface. Cover the solder area with a light coat of solder; this is called *tinning,* and the coated area will easily accept further soldering. Flux the contact area of the nut and place it on the tubing. Heat both the tube and the nut until they accept solder. If all the voids between the nut and the tube are not filled on the first try, reflux and repeat the process.

Through the center of the soldered nut, drill a ⅛-inch hole into the tube, then screw the grease fitting into the nut. The motor shaft swivels inside this tube, and grease inserted through the fitting will ensure smooth action as well as reduced vibration. The grease might also prevent water from topping the motor-shaft tube when the boat is in use.

The shorter piece of copper is the pivot tube for the tiller. It doesn't require a fitting and can be coated with grease later.

The Control Parts

Mark, set-punch, and drill—per sheet 4 (page 94)—the two 8-inch pieces of 1- × ⅛-inch bar stock. These metal pieces will be mounted on the ends of the control arm and act as a steering link. Round and smooth the ends that will be exposed.

Clamp the motor and motor shaft so you can drill a hole located 50 degrees clockwise from the rear of the shaft—viewed from the top—and ⅝ inch from the top of the shaft. Mark this location and set and drill a ⅛-inch pilot hole. Redrill this hole with a series of increasingly larger bits, working up to ⁵⁄₁₆ inch. Take *extreme care* to avoid striking the wires in the motor shaft. Shake the shavings out of the tube and set this aside.

The remainder of the control parts are wood. The pivot arm will be mounted on the motor shaft, as will the counter part of the tiller. Make these two pieces at the same time.

Draw the parts on the stock, marking and centering the positions of the holes to be drilled. Clamp the wood securely and drill the 1-inch holes, being as particular as possible to make them vertical. A drill press would be very helpful for all these drilling procedures. Drill the ⁷⁄₁₆-inch hole only ¼ inch deep, using a brad-point wood bit (a spade bit can suffice), and follow with a ¼-inch hole at the center of the shallow hole. Realign the pattern to ensure the holes are in the correct positions and cut the parts out on the bandsaw. Drill the remaining ¼-inch hole in the pivot arm and round the tiller with a ⅜-inch corner-round router bit.

Now is a good time to make the tiller block. Note that its hole is 1⅛ inches in diameter. Again, it is best to drill the hole in the stock, then cut out and finish the part.

The basic shape of the control arm is determined by the line of the hull, and it can be cut from the remaining remnant from the two bottom boards. Lay the stock along the rail from the arm brace to the stern and trace the curve of the hull onto the board. Draw a second line parallel to and 2 inches from the first one. With the bandsaw, cut out the control arm. Round all sides using a ⅜-inch corner-round bit.

Make the skeg, rounding all its edges except where it attaches to the keel. Some modification might be necessary to the skeg to conform to the type of motor used.

Make the conduit from the remnants of the keel and the motor cover plate from any suitable remaining stock. Drill all mounting holes in the conduit and the cover plate.

STEP 4: ASSEMBLING AND FINISHING

The assembly of the components is a critical part of the construction process. Take your time. Drilling the hole for the motor tube is by far the most difficult and exacting of the following procedures; the rest are only tedious.

Mounting the Motor Tube

Turn the hull over and support it at both ends across two sawhorses or the like. Sand any patches you made on the sides and bottom, and in general finish up the outside portion of the hull. Sand the last 4 inches of the keel at the stern flush with the bottom, using the belt sander to leave a radiused step up to the level of the rest of the keel. At the point at the stern where the bottom is 1¼ inches wide, mark and center a point to drill the hole for the motor tube.

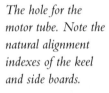

The hole for the motor tube. Note the natural alignment indexes of the keel and side boards.

You will be drilling through four different parts of the hull before the motor-tube hole exits the sternpost. Use a 1¼-inch bit, and stop at regular intervals to check for alignment. The joint between the keel and the bottom boards is your initial guide, then the juncture of the sternpost to the side boards. It is easy to see if your side-to-side alignment is correct. As for vertical alignment, the hole should be perpendicular to the bottom of the boat at the stern. Because the bit will break out of one side of the sternpost first, drilling may become difficult once this happens. It might be necessary to finish the hole with a coarse rasp. The motor-shaft tube should fit loosely through the finished hole.

Once the motor-tube hole is made, turn the boat rightside up. With a sabersaw, cut a 4-inch hole in the stern plate, centered where the stern plate is 5¾ inches wide. This should place the center of this access hole more or less over the hole for the motor-shaft tube. You might want to protect the working surface from the base of the saw with masking tape. With this hole made, you can really see what you're doing.

With the remnant of the motor shaft inside the motor tube, insert the tube into the hole flush with the bottom of the boat. Using small wedges of wood driven in place between the tube and the sternpost, adjust the tube to be perpendicular to the bottom of the boat at the stern. This is most easily accomplished by viewing the extended alignment shaft from several angles. The hole is intentionally oversize to allow for the inevitable error in drilling.

Place a machine washer and the pivot arm on the alignment shaft in the tube and check to see that the arm rotates freely, clearing the hull sides as well as the bottom of the stern plate. If this proves to be the case, proceed with the permanent installation. If the pivot arm doesn't clear the bottom of the stern plate, lower the tube in the hole until the arm works freely. If it strikes the sides of the hull, raise the tube or shift it forward.

Leaving the wedges in place, remove the pivot arm and washer and the shaft. Be sure the grease fitting in the motor tube is pointing forward. Put tape across the bottom of the motor-tube hole to keep the glue from running out, then from inside the hull inject epoxy into the void around the motor tube until all space between it and the hull is completely filled. Leave this undisturbed until the epoxy cures. You have just completed the most difficult part of building *Sam*. The rest is downhill.

Mounting the Control Arm and the Skeg

Epoxy the tiller block and the tiller tube to the bottom of the boat as shown in the first assembly drawing. The block and tube need only be weighted in place while the glue sets. Using ample flat washers under the nuts, pull the heads of two 1½-inch × ¼-inch machine bolts into the $\frac{7}{16}$-inch recesses of both the pivot arm and the tiller.

Sam's business end showing the motor without the prop, the pivot arm in place as seen through the access opening in the stern plate, and the wiring in a harness. The skeg is yet to be fitted and the wiring to be routed to the box.

Rough-up the upper surface of the tiller shaft with coarse sandpaper or a grinder and glue it into the tiller flush to the top. Make a small disk to cover the hole and glue it in place.

When the motor tube has cured, clear it of epoxy and sand the bottom flush. Install the motor, machine washer, and pivot arm (threads down). Secure the motor with a ¼-inch bolt through the pivot arm and the motor shaft, retained by a lock-nut. Do not overtighten.

Put the propeller on the motor. There should be at least ¾ inch of clearance between the prop and the stern of the boat. If not, round the stern until this clearance is reached. If it is evident that the prop simply cannot be made to clear the stern, a different prop might be necessary.

Holding the skeg against the keel, mark the portion of the fin on the motor that has to be removed. The aft tip of the skeg should be about ¾ inch forward of and in line with the tip of the prop.

Fitting the skeg depends on the type of motor you use and the prop size. Dress the surface of the skeg that mates with the keel until a good fit is achieved. Now cut away the fin of the motor at the mark; you want about ⅛ inch of clearance between the fin and the skeg. Take the motor out to make this cut if you like. The weight of the boat may at some time during use be on the skeg, and this ⅛-inch clearance will be taken up, transmitting the weight to the motor—a desirable trait lest the skeg flex too much and fail.

When all looks well, mount the skeg with 2½-inch and 2-inch brass screws

The motor and skeg in place. Note the proximity of the motor fin and the prop to the skeg. Note also that the patches over the screw holes in the side board are small because of the use of washers.

flush through the top of the keel. Drill one hole as far to the rear as possible while remaining accessible; the stern plate will interfere with access if the screw is placed too far aft. Drill the hole for the shorter screw as far forward as possible without risking the screw running through the skeg. Countersink both holes and pilot-drill the skeg. When you are satisfied with the fit, bed the screws in a gasket sealant—not one containing silicone—and tighten. When you need to remove the motor later, remove the front screw only and simply rotate the skeg to the side.

Place a machine washer on the tiller shaft and insert the tiller assembly into the tiller tube. Using a washer and a standard nut, mount one control-arm end to the pivot arm and one to the tiller. Align both the motor and the tiller to the straight forward position and tighten the nuts to hold the arms steady. Place the wooden control arm over the end attached to the tiller and under the end at the pivot, and mark the locations of the ends on the wood. Remove the ends and mount them on the control arm with ¾-inch sheet-metal screws. Install the control-arm assembly and check for alignment and rotation of the motor. Some bending of the metal ends may be necessary to assure smooth operation. Some spacing with washers at the pivot bolts may also be required. When all works as it should, glue and screw the ends to the control arm.

The degree of rotation of the motor is a fine point. If it is too small, tight turns will be difficult. If it is too great, the motor stands out and there is a good chance of its being snagged, usually resulting in damage to the pivot arm. A good rule of thumb is to have the motor rotate so that its head doesn't stand out from the line of the hull. This can be limited by a small adjustment in the length of the wooden portion of the control arm.

Wiring

Hopefully your motor has only one switch that allows for both forward and reverse operation. If not, the following still applies, just twofold. Most likely the switch shaft won't be quite long enough to go through the seat box. Using an appropriate bit, drill a recess for the mounting nut on the outside of the seat box; mount the switch as close to the seat back as possible and low enough to allow the lid to lie flat after all wires are attached. This should fall in a good location for the right hand, operating by feel only.

A note here for those who might wish to deviate from the seat-box plan. The seat box as drawn is simply a place for the battery and the switches and maybe a few items of storage that can stand that environment. It need not be so basic. The switches can be relocated or removed from the box altogether and the box partitioned to provide a wet or dry well. You can make any other modifications you wish; it's up to you.

Mount the conduit piece on the centerline of the boat with the square end against the back of the seat box and the 45-degree end at the rear. Now take it back up and drill a ½-inch hole in the seat box in line with the channel in the conduit. Pull at least one of the wires from the motor through this hole and replace the conduit with the wire in the channel. Route the wire along the base edge of the seat box and up to the switch. If it is too short, add a piece that makes the length plus 6 inches. Remove the conduit again and splice additional length onto the rest of the wires from the motor, using the appropriate-size wire (see Appendix B) and, if possible, the same color. Solder the splices, using the correct-size unsheathed barrel connectors, and stagger them so they won't all be in the same place in the harness. Tape each connection lightly.

Starting at the motor, tightly wrap all the wires together with electrical tape to form a harness. Route the harness to the switch and install the conduit over it to cover the harness from the seat box to the post. Inside the seat box, route the harness to the sides, out of the way of the battery. Trim the wires to the right length, install the appropriate connectors, and connect the wires to the switch. Shorten the battery leads, if necessary, and also connect them to the switch.

Install the battery. Set the switch to the full-speed position, then touch the battery clamps to the battery terminal, prepared to remove them quickly if the motor fails to turn yet there is a spark at the terminal. If the motor happens to be wired improperly, the speed-control coil could be damaged if connected to the battery too long. Test briefly in all speeds and reverse. If all is well, move on; if not, rethink the wiring. Remove the battery after testing.

Install the seat-box lid with the pair of brass hinges at the rear. Center the motor cover plate over the access hole and install it with three brass screws. *Sam* is now completely assembled and *in the white*, or unfinished. Now take it back apart and set aside the motor assembly and the switch.

Finishing

Before you are eight separate wooden parts: hull, seat-box lid, tiller, control arm, motor cover plate, conduit, skeg, and pivot arm. All that is left to do is to seal and finish the wood. You will have a mandatory break coming very soon, so hang in there.

Easier said than done, sand all wooden parts. Most of the rough sanding on the bottom is already done. Use 80-grit paper on areas that are very rough, then 120-grit on everything to finish. This is a good place for a palm sander, but don't try finish-sanding with a belt or a disk sander.

Chip or sand away excess glue. Sand out pilot burns and any other marks. Make sure the backrest is smooth. If you wish, you can sit in the boat by placing it on several thick blankets on a level surface; step in with clean feet and place pressure on the keel only. Get the seat the way you want it by shaping the back; this is where you can use a disc sander, but finish with a palm sander or by hand. When everything is sanded, clean the work and the shop thoroughly of dust. Set all wooden parts in easy reach and prepare to seal the wood.

Gluvit is great stuff once you know how to use it. Learning how has taken me years, and I'm still learning. The objective is to close the grain of the wood and provide a smooth finish, using only enough material to do the job. Too much and there will be the most aggravating brush strokes to be removed. Too little and the wood might not be properly protected. Proper application requires advance planning and patience.

Start with the hull bottomside up and all other parts close at hand. I prefer a 2-inch brush, and it need not be top quality. Gloves are essential, and a mask is a good idea. Not enough can be said about precautions: Ventilate the shop to the max; follow label instructions; no open flames.

Mix ¾ of a quart can per label instructions. Cut this 50/50 with thinner; lacquer thinner will do. Mix well initially and mix frequently during use to avoid settling. As the mixture is applied to the wood, the solvent quickly evaporates. If the brush starts to drag, reload it and move on. Some areas of the wood will soak up more than others; go back over any "dry" areas. As you work, the mixture might need additional thinning to replace the solvent that evaporates. If brush strokes start to appear, the thinner is flashing off; reload the brush with thinner-rich Gluvit and move on. Get the nooks and crannies first, then work the flats and the large areas. Avoid slopping on the sealer as this can lead to uneven areas of color.

You will need someone in the wings to help you turn the boat. Tack four wooden blocks covered with waxed paper to the work table and rest the bottom on these. Touch up any areas handled while turning the hull.

Do not feel you have to use every last bit of the mixture. When a place looks like it's done, don't come back and try to cover it again or touch it up. You are looking for an even, matte finish. Very dull areas need more sealer and glossy areas have more than enough. You will probably have some visible brush strokes, but work at keeping them to a minimum.

Make sure you don't forget any of the parts. When you've done all you can do, close the shop and take yourself outside for plenty of fresh air.

Gluvit, like other epoxies, cures by time at temperature; the warmer the shop, the quicker the cure. In the summer weather where I live—90°F days and 60°F nights—sanding can start again in three to four days. In the winter, even with the shop heater going full blast, it usually takes a week. (If yours is a flame heater, ventilate the shop *for several hours* after application before you fire it up.) The longer you give the epoxy to cure, the crisper it will sand. Give it time; when it's ready— you'll know by the way it sands. Prepare to smooth it down. This can be done wet or dry with 180- or 220-grit paper. The correct sandpaper for finishing is wet-or-dry carbide. I use carbide paper for bare wood as well, mostly 100-grit, and I buy it in rolls—called *floor-sanding paper.*

I prefer to wet-sand the Gluvit surface. This goes a lot faster than sanding bare wood; you're now working on a synthetic surface. Be careful not to sand through the epoxy on the sharp edges or they will show up badly after the varnish. Check your work frequently by wiping it down and feeling for rough areas. Get a friend to help—this part can be fun.

When all the sanding is finished, install the motor, the washer and pivot arm, and the skeg. Remove the rag placed in the motor shaft earlier. The motor must be allowed to breath; do not obstruct this passage. Install the switch and the conduit. Do not install the cover plate, control arm, or tiller. Again, wipe everything down with

A view of Sam *from the bottom during varnishing.*

a tack rag and get the shop as dust-free as possible. Even better would be to relocate the work to a dust-free environment if you can find one. Dust is the worst enemy of a good varnish job.

Taking all possible precautions against dust, proceed to varnish the boat. Use the varnish as it comes from the can; do not thin it. For varnish you need a high-quality brush—new or perfectly clean; a 2-inch width is about right. Do not go back to touch up varnish; get it right the first time. Feather out the varnish as you move down the work surface, taking care not to overload overlap areas. Always stroke the brush out of the varnish, not back into the previously coated area. Have plenty of good light and, if you can, have a friend spot for you. This is a great help in catching missed areas or runs before it is too late to correct them. On a good day the surface of the varnish will be dry enough after 4 to 6 hours not to catch dust. A dry day is preferred, but unfortunately dry days promote dust whereas wet days don't. It will not be easy to get a dust-free finish, but this is only the first coat.

Give the varnish a few days to dry, then install the lid, motor cover plate, control arm, and tiller. With a combination of flat washers and lock washers, tighten the tiller-to-control-arm bolt to where the tiller is easy to move but has to overcome some friction. This will keep the motor in line when your hand isn't on the tiller. The pivot-to-control-arm bolt should be set up more loosely, leaving some play between the two parts.

Hand-grease the tiller tube; the tiller simply lifts out, making this task easy. Use a grease gun to fill the motor tube, rotating the motor side to side while filling.

TRIAL RUN

This is the long-awaited day. *Sam,* or whatever your boat's name is now, is best launched from a beach. Place the boat—without the battery—into the water and snug the nose to the beach. Never carry or load the boat with the battery on board. This first time, take off your shoes and wade out to install the battery. Later you'll learn to do this without getting out of your shoes. Make sure the switch is *off* and connect the battery leads. To verify that the leads are making good contact, see if the motor responds when switched to low speed. Load the boat with at least a paddle and life vest. Add a towel to wipe up water from your feet or the paddle. Avoid taking a passenger right now; testing is a very important step in building a boat and demands concentration.

Wipe the boat clean and dry of all water on the inside. Get in and get acquainted. Push off a short distance and study all the seams in sight. There might be a place you expected a leak; study it. If all looks good, turn on the power. Check to see that all speeds are working, as well as reverse. Is the tiller moving too freely or does it need another turn on the adjustment nut? If you stay out an hour or so and

A completed boat on display at the North Carolina Maritime Museum. This boat is actually a Black River Guide, similar in many ways to Sam.

there's no sign of water in the boat, your testing is done. When you get the boat back to its rack, before even wiping it down, always put the battery on the charger. Recharging as soon as possible after use will ensure long life for the battery, and your electric boat will always be ready for your next outing. Do not overcharge—this severely shortens the life of your battery. If your charger is self-regulating, minimum supervision is needed; if it isn't, monitor your recharging carefully.

You are now an electric boater. This is a good time to give the boat that final coat of varnish that will make it the pride of the neighborhood. You've built a boat that you can build again if so desired. You can also repair most any part of your boat since you made the parts. Maybe you can get that friend who helped you in the shop with your boat to make one too; it's a lot more fun with someone else riding alongside your rail.

SUMMARY

The boat described above lacks some of the features described in earlier chapters, features like PWM speed control and in-tiller controls. Their absence will not detract greatly from the use and enjoyment of this simple craft, while including them can make construction much more difficult.

In the chapter that follows, you will find a list of current electric-boat builders, some of whom offer plans or parts for conversion to electrical propulsion.

CHAPTER 10

ELECTRIC BOATS
YOU CAN BUY

ELECTRIC BOATS HAVE BEEN AROUND FOR SOME TIME. The first outboard motor, built in 1881, was electric. In 1893, at the World Columbian Exposition in Chicago, a fleet of 55 launches, each 36 feet long and built by the Electric Launch Company (later shortened to Elco), were used in passenger service to demonstrate the marvels of electricity. Electric propulsion remained almost exclusively the province of large, opulent launches during the early and mid 1900s. More recently, improvements in magnet technology and the development of submersible electric motors have converted many average anglers to electric boaters. Though small and inconspicuous, electric trolling motors ply streams and lakes everywhere, affording most everyone the quiet of electric propulsion.

The availability and simplicity of installation of electric outboards make converting a boat originally propelled by a fossil-fuel outboard relatively easy. Conversion from inboard gasoline or diesel power to electric propulsion is almost always less than satisfactory. The success of an electric boat is due largely to its overall design, where batteries also serve as ballast, controls are appropriate for the electric propulsion, and hull design is suited to low power and relatively low speeds. Most conversions are likely to result in a dramatic reduction in power and speed, not in keeping with the boat's original design purpose or the owner's intended use.

That electric boats really are different from most other craft makes conversion, in most cases, inappropriate (a possible exception being the simple expedient of mounting a trolling motor on an easily propelled canoe). Their usually efficient

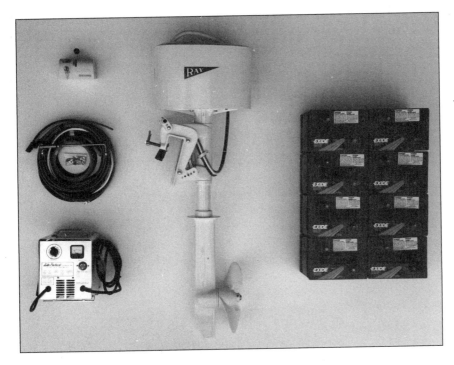

The powerful Ray Electric outboard is an alternative to the fossil-fuel engine. (Photo courtesy Ray Electric)

displacement hulls and fine lines, their attention to detail, and their quiet operation make true electric boats quite distinct from ordinary runabouts. Increasing interest in electric boats has prompted the founding of the Electric Boat Association of America (see pages 128–129).

Today, electric boats occupy a unique niche in the overall boating market. Following is a survey of popular models of electric boats made in the U.S. The technical data as provided by the builders is presented in a consistent format. Weights or displacements given include battery banks except when stated otherwise. Speeds and ranges depend upon how the craft is operated.

THE TRADITIONAL LAUNCH

In the realm of electric boats, the launch is probably the most expected form. The very nature of boating for pleasure embraces electric propulsion's most outstanding features and easily accommodates its eccentricities. Launches are most often used on waters where restrictions on wake, speed, or the fossil-fuel engine are in effect. They are as at home at the dock accepting a charge and stating their elegance as they are slipping silently around a harbor or shuttling among lakeside homes. Though their

THE ELECTRIC BOAT ASSOCIATION OF AMERICA (EBAA)

The following is excerpted from a letter from the founder of the EBAA outlining the organization's guidelines and goals:

The Electric Boat Association of America (EBAA) was founded in 1992 . . . to promote electric boating in this country. Clear needs and areas in which such an association could be effective . . . were identified and defined:

- *We need a voice.*
- *We need a core.*
- *We need a venue for ideas.*
- *We need our own organization to help take us into the future—an era when alternatives will be sought, even demanded and welcomed.*
- *We need representation: in Washington, in the state capitals, in the press, and in the minds of the public. We need representation wherever boating and energy and environment are being discussed.*
- *We need an educational arm and a central informational source for others— including the press—to learn about electric boating.*
- *We need a medium for communication among ourselves.*
- *We need a place where meetings and symposia and tests and regattas and just plain fun can be planned and organized.*
- *We need a clearing house for our ideas and products and discoveries.*
- *We need a center for communicating with universities and laboratories and other places where scientific advances in the field of electric power and energy storage are being made.*
- *We need a link with like-minded people who are focused on electric-powered vehicles for use on land.*
- *We need to communicate with people in other countries interested in electric boating, related products, and scientific advances.*

hulls may range from efficient to fair, their accommodations are rarely lacking, and range is seldom a factor as time spent aboard can be enjoyed even if sitting still. Brightly colored canopies and pennants add to the easygoing nature of these craft.

Though a basic configuration is the norm, some launches offer accessory items

From the start, it was stressed that the EBAA was to be an organization to encourage and celebrate electric-powered boating as it is known today. While EBAA is vitally interested in technological advances that will make the boating activity more attractive to more people, the association believes that electric boats are quite satisfactory the way they are. Members are not sitting back and waiting for some monumental breakthrough—as seems to be the case, for instance, with electric automobiles. They are already, perhaps, even a little smug with the notion that their electric boats are so easy to maintain: no tune-ups, no carburetors, no cooling fluids.

In the area of technology, EBAA works for scientific advances, including alternative sources of energy, but that is not the principal mission. The same holds true in the area of environmental protection. Electric-powered boating is certainly kinder to the environment than any other form of propulsion in use today. Electric boats don't go fast enough to disturb the shorelines, annoy others, or injure the flora and fauna. They don't smoke or stink or put petroleum in the water. (They don't put petroleum anywhere—a substance that contributes in a major way to the U.S. trade imbalance and budget deficit.)

EBAA is not primarily an environmental protection outfit, but communications have been established with most of the major environmental groups in North America, and EBAA has received their blessing and support.

What of the future? It really depends on the association's ability to attract enough members to become a truly self-sustaining organization; to be able to communicate more widely and in greater depth; to make the advantages of its kind of leisure activity, and to encourage and utilize technological advances.

If you are interested in the organization, contact:

Ken Matthews
Electric Boat Association of America
P.O. Box 11197
Naples, Florida 33941
(813) 774-3773

such as additional battery capacity, modest photovoltaics, and even generators. Their systems are generally designed for the environment in which they find greatest acceptance. Many boats of this type are made outside the continental U.S. They are especially popular in England and Scandinavian countries.

Elco

Elco got its start in 1893 with the 36-foot launch. By 1917 Elco was building 80-foot motor launches for the British war effort. Elco had by then built some 1,000 electric pleasure boats, and although they continued to build electric boats after 1917, the majority of the company's energy was employed in government contracts for freighters, sub chasers, and other nonelectric vessels. During the 1940s Elco built 399 PT boats, one of which was John F. Kennedy's PT 109. After the war the shop set about doing custom woodworking as business declined. In 1949 Elco was liquidated, and in 1952 the Elco name was dropped from the conglomerate empire of General Dynamics.

In June of 1987, Elco was reestablished under the hand of Joseph Fleming, Jr. The first project was a classic 30-foot "Fantail" launch modeled after the *Diana E. Banks*. This cold-molded wood vessel departed from the electric launches of earlier years with a modern, state-of-the-art electrical system. The new 30-foot launch made its debut in January 1988 at the Miami International Boat Show.

Today Elco offers electric launches in 21-, 24-, and 30-foot versions. With particular attention to traditional appearance and detail, Elco builds some of the finest electric boats currently being manufactured; accordingly, they are also among the most expensive. Many options are available.

The Classic Elco 30 has a six- to eight-person capacity at a price of $63,000. Its fiberglass hull is 30 feet 6 inches long by 6 feet 6 inches wide. It draws 29 inches and displaces 5,000 pounds. The inboard 48-volt 5-h.p. field-wound motor turns at 1,600 rpm, spinning a 15 × 14 three-blade propeller through a 2:1 reduction

The Elco 30-foot electric launch. (Photo courtesy Elco)

drive. Electrical power is stored in eight 220-Ah 12-volt batteries and delivered by a solid-state variable speed control. An onboard charger is fitted. Speed and range are 6.3 mph for 12 hours.

Electra Craft

Electra Craft offers a variety of electrically propelled boats from 10 to 21 feet in length. The California-based company, established in 1975, is a major U.S. builder of electric boats that fit the lifestyles of waterfront-home owners on residential lakes, harbors, and inland waterways. Five-knot speed limits and prohibitions against gasoline-powered boats have contributed to the popularity of Electra Craft and other boats using electric power. For this market Electra Craft offers many of the extras that an electric vessel can so easily accommodate—such features as an AC/DC inverter, dome light, battery-condition indicator, and sound system, to list a few. The traditional appearance and convenient size make the 16-foot model one of the most popular of the Electra Craft line.

The Bay Cruiser 16 has a six- to eight-person capacity at a price of $11,995. Its fiberglass hull is 16 feet by 6 feet 8 inches. It draws 20 inches and weighs 1,650 pounds. The inboard 36-volt 3-h.p. permanent-magnet motor turns at 2,150 rpm, spinning an 11 × 8 three-blade propeller through a reduction drive. Electrical power is stored in six 220-Ah 6-volt batteries and delivered by a solid-state variable speed control. An onboard charger is fitted. Speed and range are 5.7 mph for 8 hours.

Duffield Electric Boat Company

The Duffield Electric Boat Company offers 16-, 18-, and 21-foot electrically propelled boats from its California shop. All are built in the tradition of the elegant launches to which Southern California is accustomed. Established in 1970, Duffield

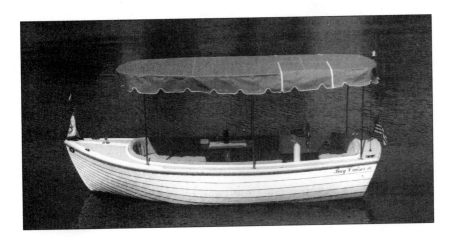

The Electra Craft Bay Cruiser 16. (Photo courtesy Electra Craft)

builds boats representative of the typical craft for residential lakes and restricted waters. As with other pleasure boats of their class, Duffield boats offer many options to enhance comfort and appearance. These include refrigeration, depthfinder, electric anchor windlass, and added ballast for additional stability. The Duffy 18 is one of Duffield's more popular boats.

The Duffy 18 has a six- to eight-person capacity at a price of $13,195. Its fiberglass hull is 18 feet by 6 feet 6 inches. It draws 23 inches at a weight of 1,700 pounds. The inboard 36-volt 3-h.p. field-wound motor turns at 1,700 rpm, spinning a 15 X 15 three-blade propeller through a 2:1 reduction. Electrical storage is provided by six 220-Ah 6-volt batteries, with power delivered through a solid-state variable speed control. An onboard charger is standard. Speed and range are 4 mph for 8 hours.

Beckmann

Beckmann's Rhode Island company offers a variety of watercraft, all based on traditional themes, which include steam, diesel, antique gas, and electric power systems. Beckmann also offers components, custom building, hulls, and kits. Their electric boats range from 17 to 25 feet, with many options available on the typical classic launch.

The Rose 20 has a four-person capacity at a price of $13,950. Its fiberglass hull is 20 feet by 4 feet 4 inches. It draws 20 inches and weighs 1,000 pounds. The inboard 36-volt 1.5-h.p. field-wound motor turns at 2,800 rpm, spinning a 20 X 30 three-blade propeller through a 10:1 reduction. Electrical power is stored in six 220-Ah 6-volt batteries and delivered by a solid-state variable speed control. An onboard charger is fitted. Speed and range are 4 mph for 6 hours.

Rose 20.
*(Photo courtesy
Beckmann Ltd.)*

Budsin Woodcraft

With the increased interest in electric propulsion for craft operating in restricted waters, Budsin has recently built a number of attractive wooden boats—up to 26 feet long—with many of the characteristics of the classic launch. Being a custom builder, Budsin can make many options available to the prospective buyer. As with most woodworkers, Budsin gives great attention to detail and appearance, with extensive use of mahogany finished bright. This is evident in the Lightning Bug.

The Lightning Bug has a four-person capacity at a price of $9,350. Its 15-foot

*Lightning Bug.
(Photo courtesy
Budsin Woodcraft)*

ELECTRIC BOATS YOU CAN BUY

by 4-foot-2-inch cold-molded white-cedar hull draws 13 inches and weighs 300 pounds. The inboard 24-volt 0.5-h.p. 1,125-rpm permanent-magnet motor provides direct drive to a 9 × 4 three-blade propeller. Electrical power is stored in two 115-Ah 12-volt batteries and delivered by a solid-state variable speed control. The boat is equipped with an onboard charger. Speed and range are 3.5 mph for 5 hours.

Ray Electric

Ray Electric has been a builder of primary-power electric outboard motors since 1973. Ray's motors are some of the most suitable outboards for easy conversion from gas to electrical propulsion. The company has now coupled the powerful and versatile Ray Electric outboard with a hull designed for electric propulsion to create the Ray Electric Explorer. The Explorer offers the union of a proven electric propulsion unit in a displacement craft with excellent characteristics for range, speed, and comfort. Building from the prop up, this Florida company has a great deal of experience with its product. Options include refrigeration, solar panels for primary replenishment, and an onboard 1,000-watt generator. The long, narrow lines and shallow draft of the Explorer make for a good river cruiser.

Ray Electric Explorer. (Photo courtesy Ray Electric)

The Ray Electric Explorer has a six- to eight-person capacity at a price of $14,000. Its fiberglass hull is 21 feet by 5 feet 6 inches. The boat draws 16 inches and weighs 1,200 pounds. The above-water outboard has a 48-volt 3.5-h.p. field-wound motor operating at up to 3,100 rpm; it spins a 12½ × 10 two-blade propeller through a 3:1 reduction drive. Electrical power is provided by eight 235-Ah 6-volt batteries and delivered through a solid-state PWM speed control. An onboard charger is standard. Speed and range are 7.5 mph for 8 hours.

THE ELECTRIC CANOE
AND SMALL FISHING BOATS

Electric propulsion for small, canoelike boats is only now gaining the acceptance that is long overdue. The ability to travel in silence with precise control has always been the tradition of the canoe, and now the option of electric propulsion adds a new dimension for boaters wanting to trade their paddle for a camera or field glasses.

There is little difference between an electric canoe and its traditional counterpart. The electric canoe can still be paddled, though this is a rare occurrence once the operator is familiar with electric propulsion. Range and speed are more of a factor in the electric canoe than in larger electric boats. Because electric canoes are frequently operated in shallow backwaters or on swift and snaggy creeks, they must be rugged and have a shallow draft; they should be tough enough to drag across debris or shallow areas. Electric canoes, with batteries removed, can be cartopped or carried in a truck bed.

Many accessories are available for the electric canoe, including photovoltaics and generators. Though usually barebones, these electric boats, above all others, ought to have instrumentation and a covered well for ice, water, or protection of gear from the elements. Their range for their size is considerable, and their capacity may be as much as five times their empty weight.

Black River Boats

Located on the headwaters of the Black River in eastern North Carolina, Black River Boats offers four models from 12 to 16 feet made explicitly for backwater use. The matched planks of Atlantic white cedar with black walnut keel and rails make for an attractive yet rugged electric boat. Established in 1985, Black River has concentrated on boats featuring low profile, shallow draft, and good speed and range. These boats are at home in swamps and swift shallow creeks or just as comfortable being displayed for their attractive appearance. Full instrumentation is standard on 16-foot models, in-tiller controls on others.

The Black River Companion has a two-person capacity at a price of $2,950. Its 15-foot-11-inch by 32-inch white-cedar hull draws 8 inches at a weight of 105 pounds without batteries. The submersible 12-volt 0.5-h.p. permanent-magnet motor turns at 1,200 rpm direct to a 7 × 4 three-blade propeller. Electrical storage is provided by two 135-Ah 12-volt batteries, with the power delivered through a solid state speed control. Speed and range are 3.5 mph for 12 hours.

SOLAR STRIDER

Curtis and Kathleen Saville have accomplished what some would see as quite remarkable: they have traveled the equivalent distance of an Atlantic crossing in a solar-powered boat. This is no small feat considering the inherent characteristics of solar power and the distance involved.

Their attempt to *actually* cross the Atlantic Ocean was interrupted off the coast of Africa, where the original craft was destroyed in a sudden and violent storm. Salvaging what they could of photovoltaics and related equipment, they set about finding a replacement to continue on kinder waters their quest of traveling on solar power a distance equivalent to an Atlantic crossing. The North Carolina Maritime Museum led the Savilles to our shop, where Curtis explained their plan and needs.

It was our combined good fortune that *Strider* was on the rack for sale. *Strider* was a year old and had seen many hours of use and evaluation. It was built to incorporate as many features for efficient operation as possible in a quest for range. It had seen both good times and the not so pleasant, as it was pushed hard and long to find its shortcomings. It could tote a load and take it a long way, and it never failed in its many hours of operation. The 16-foot by 30-inch white-cedar hull had less rocker than our other boats, which made it fast but less accommodating to beach or handle shallow water. All *Strider*'s features seemed to be desirable in a boat using the relatively small amount of power supplied by solar conversion, and any backwater characteristic it lacked would rarely be missed. With a 24-volt system in place, the Savilles took *Strider* away to adapt the salvaged photovoltaics and controls to what was to become *Solar Strider*.

Solar Strider *on a run down the Northeast Cape Fear River. (Photo courtesy Curtis Saville)*

As it is set up now, *Solar Strider* is outfitted with two 12-volt PV panels aligned in series to charge a pair of 35-Ah 24-volt batteries through a 24-volt charge controller. A Curtis speed control is mounted on the back side of the storage compartment, with the potentiometer brought forward on a tether to the tiller. *Solar Strider*'s range is 15 miles on one pair of batteries or 30 with an additional pair stored forward. The solar bank at the Savilles' house can charge the pair of batteries in a day; the panels on the boat may require a week. The 24-volt motor turns a three-blade 7-inch prop and produces about 40 pounds of thrust, drawing about 16 amps at top speed.

Electra-Ghost Canoes

The increasing awareness and interest in the environment have prompted a corresponding interest in and demand for small, portable, electrically propelled boats. Alan Cady has recently started building such a craft in his Maryland shop. The Electra-Ghost Whisper is an ideal vessel for the naturalist or photographer to use in backwater creeks where wildlife is most prevalent. The Whisper is offered with such options as cane-back seats and ash coamings.

Whisper.
(Photo courtesy
Electra-Ghost)

The Whisper has a two- to three-person capacity at a price of $2,950. Its 18-foot by 38-inch fiberglass hull draws 12 inches and weighs 105 pounds without batteries. The submersible 12-volt 0.45-h.p. permanent-magnet motor turns at 1,100 rpm direct to a 9 × 4 two-blade propeller. Electrical storage is in two 210-RAC 12-volt batteries, with the supply controlled by a solid-state variable speed control. Speed and range are 3 mph for 15 hours.

Crow Boats

With the fisherman in mind, Crow Boats offers several boats with electric propulsion. Their boats are reasonable in price and commonly found on the rivers of North Carolina, where the company is located. Though the electric propulsion system is an add-on, it is installed and fitted in such a manner as to create a true electric boat. Steering is by foot pedal, and the one- and two-person models are the most popular of these electric fishing boats. Built for the close control at low speeds required for fishing, their high and comfortable profile makes them good for lake and river use.

One-Man Crow. (Photo courtesy Crow Boats)

The one-man Crow holds one person and is priced at $675 without a battery. Its 10-foot-8-inch by 38-inch ABS-plastic hull draws 12 inches and weighs 75 pounds without the battery. The submersible 12-volt 0.41-h.p. permanent-magnet motor turns at 1,100 rpm direct to a 9 × 4 two-blade propeller. A single 115-Ah 12-volt battery supplies the electrical power, controlled by a rheostat speed control. Speed and range are 4 mph for 3 hours.

A CANAL BOAT

A canal boat is an ideal platform for the massive systems of the electric boat. Speed and range can be of secondary importance to comfort and stability. The canal boat can be a home away from home that has the space and displacement for many options. These electric boats have long been popular in Europe for use on canals and restricted waters.

MOG Canal Boats

George and Hillary McNeir have thrown themselves into building what they call their MOG Canal Boat. This application of electrical propulsion coupled with a generator and extensive photovoltaics produces an independent vessel ideal for those wanting to slip away to enjoy some quiet backwater estuary. Depending upon how it's operated, MOG can be entirely self-sustaining. At this time only one MOG has been built, but the McNeirs are optimistic that their boat will find popularity among those who desire the unique qualities it has to offer.

MOG.
(Photo courtesy MOG Canal Boats)

MOG (prototype) can house a family at a price of $160,000. Its wooden hull is 30 feet by 11 feet 6 inches. It draws 24 inches and has a displacement of 11,000 pounds. Twin inboard 48-volt 5-h.p. field-wound motors turn at 1,600 rpm direct to a pair of 12 × 11 three-blade propellers. Electrical storage is handled by two banks of eight 200-Ah 6-volt batteries, and the power is delivered through a solid-state speed control. The boat is equipped with a 4.5-kW onboard generator and 1.5 kW of photovoltaics. Speed and range are 4 mph for 5 hours a day for 8 days—without sun or use of the generator.

IN CLOSING

My most sincere thanks to those electric-boat builders who have contributed technical information for use in this book. To those who are designing and building electrically propelled boats, may these contributions prove of value.

There are many who are active in expanding the virtues of the electric boat through the use of photovoltaics and other new ideas. Most boatbuilders have started

(text continues on page 142)

THE MOG CANAL BOAT

The distinct advantage electrically propelled watercraft have over their land-based counterparts is their ability to carry greater loads at acceptable speeds. The MOG Canal Boat takes advantage of the many attributes of electricity to provide a water-based home-away-from-home that can be self-sustained by photovoltaics. Its 24-inch draft allows for the exploration of backwater estuaries for as long as one may wish to stay, and MOG is environmentally friendly, from its silent electrical system to its composting toilet.

The use of the sun to power a boat is practical to a point, the point where the demand for propulsion power exceeds the capacity of the photovoltaics. With MOG's large surface area for solar collection and acceptable low speed, a balance may be reached where solar power is all that is necessary. According to builder George McNeir, the 140 square feet of photovoltaics captures some 1,200 watts of clean energy every sunny hour, which is stored in a battery bank for use at the discretion of the operator. This 20 kWh of stored energy is the fuel tank that supplies the 7.5-kW propulsion system and all electrical accessories.

(continued on following page)

Interior of the MOG Canal Boat viewed from the main salon looking forward to the operator's station. (Photo courtesy MOG Canal Boats)

In the event of poor solar days or large demands in propulsion (adverse winds or currents), MOG is equipped with a 4.5-kW gasoline-powered generator. The generator can be used when not at dockside for battery charging or operating high-demand appliances. Recharging at dockside is possible through the 220-/120-volt AC hook-up.

The cruising speed of this 30-foot canal boat is 3.5 knots, with a top speed of 7 knots. The interior is given a feel of spaciousness through the generous use of windows. Two hundred square feet of living space accommodates a galley with a full sink, a two-burner propane stove with oven, and a refrigerator; a head with a 30- by 30-inch shower stall, a standard-size toilet, a sink, and a vanity; a stateroom with a queen-size bed; and a main salon with two 78-inch berths. All head-room is 7 feet.

MOG is a boat for those wanting the comforts of a large boat and the shallow-draft capability and quiet operating characteristics of an electric boat. The balance of photovoltaics, auxiliary generation, and creature comforts makes this boat unique. It is not a boat for speed and is not intended to be. Its range is a function of its operation, and with the accommodations and comforts aboard, there is little need to be in a hurry, little else to do but enjoy and appreciate the pleasures of the craft and the beauty of the places it can go with minimum impact on the environment.

and many succeeded by building boats for their local waters—waters they traveled in boats they built and improved upon until one day those boats had their own identity. Such an identity is usually associated with the local area or environment in which the builder has become expert in his craft.

To the backyard builder I say, "Think electric." One can be as creative or modest as he or she wishes with electric propulsion systems. There are areas such as photovoltaics and hybrid systems with which to experiment. Don't be overwhelmed by the batteries. Think of them as heavy fuel tanks or good ballast. Sure, without a recharge, on board or off, most electric boats won't go very far for very long, but be realistic about how long they are likely to be used at any one time: usually not longer than a reasonable reserve capacity permits.

Before discovering electric propulsion, how to use and build a canoe was all I cared to know about boats. It didn't take long for me to recognize how great electric boats truly are. The electric canoe, for example, so far exceeds the performance of its paddled cousin that comparisons are difficult. The control, the power, the quiet, the freedom to use one's hands—these must be experienced to be appreciated. But once experienced, even the most die-hard paddlers may get hooked on electric boats—just as I am. And to those whose boating has been accompanied by the din and unconscionable pollution of the two-cycle outboard, I say give the clean, quiet alternative a try; you might thank me. I know the planet will.

DIRECTORY
OF SUPPLIERS

ASSOCIATIONS

Electric Boat Association of America
P.O. Box 11197
Naples, FL 33941
(813) 774-3773

BOATBUILDERS

Joseph Fleming III
Electric Launch Company, Inc.
261 Upper N. Road
Highland, NY 12528
(914) 691-3777

Skip Toller
Electra Craft
31265-B La Baya Dr.
Westlake Village, CA 91382
(800) 221-2083

Gary Crane
Duffield Electric Boat Company
670 W. 17th Street, Suite D-2

Costa Mesa, CA 92627
(714) 645-6812

Walter Beckmann
Beckmann Ltd.
P.O. Box 97
Wakefield, RI 02280-0097
(401) 783-1859

Tom Hesselink
Budsin Woodcraft
P.O. Box 279
Marshallberg, NC 28553
(919) 729-1540

Morton Ray
Ray Electric
908 N.E. 24th Lane, Unit 6
Cape Coral, FL 33909-2915
(813) 574-1948

Douglas Little
Black River Boats
Route 1 Box 173 D

Rose Hill, NC 28458
(910) 532-4217

Allen B. Cady
Electra-Ghost Canoes
7117 Bembe Beach Road
Annapolis, MD 21403
(410) 268-1808

Linwood Stone
Crow Boats, Inc.
P.O. Box 1557
Lumberton, NC 28358
(800) 334-5211

George McNeir III
MOG Canal Boats
P.O. Box 1003
Wrightsville Beach, NC 28480-1003
(919) 686-1605

MOTORS

Ray Electric
908 N.E. 24th Lane, Unit 6
Cape Coral, FL 33909-2915

General Electric
3135 Easton Turnpike
Fairfield, CT 06432

Baldour Electric Co.
5711 S 7th Street
Ft. Smith, AR 72901

Johnson Fishing, Inc.
1531 Madison Avenue
Mankato, MN 56001

MotorGuide
Box 270
Tulsa, OK 74101

SPEED CONTROLS, INSTRUMENTS, ETC.

Beckmann Ltd.
P.O. Box 97
Wakefield, RI 02280-0097

Elco
261 Upper N. Road
Highland, NY 12528

Ray Electric
908 N.E. 24th Lane, Unit 6
Cape Coral, FL 33909-2915

Curtis Instruments, Inc.
200 Kisco Avenue
Mt. Kisco, NY 10549

Johnson Fishing, Inc.
1531 Madison Avenue
Mankato, MN 56001

BATTERIES, GENERATORS, AND PVS

Roberts Brothers Motors, Inc.
P.O. Box 59
Athens, TN 37303
(615) 745-0861

Hamilton Ferris
P.O. Box 126
Ashland, MA 01721

Real Goods
966 Mazzoni St.
Ukiah, CA 95482-3471

CONDUCTOR SIZES FOR 3-PERCENT DROP IN VOLTAGE

(Total current on circuit in amps.) (Length of conductor from source of current to device and back to source—feet)

12 volts

amps	10	15	20	25	30	40	50	60	70	80	90	100	110	120	130	140	150	160	170
5	18	16	14	12	12	10	10	10	8	8	8	6	6	6	6	6	6	6	6
10	14	12	10	10	10	8	6	6	6	6	4	4	4	2	2	2	2	2	2
15	12	10	10	8	8	6	6	6	4	4	2	2	2	2	1	1	1	1	1
20	10	10	8	6	6	6	4	4	2	2	2	2	1	1	1	0	0	0	2/0
25	10	8	6	6	6	4	4	2	2	2	1	1	0	0	0	2/0	2/0	2/0	3/0
30	10	8	6	6	4	4	2	2	1	1	0	0	2/0	2/0	3/0	3/0	3/0	3/0	3/0
40	8	6	6	4	4	2	2	1	0	0	2/0	2/0	3/0	3/0	3/0	4/0	4/0	4/0	4/0
50	6	6	4	4	2	2	1	0	2/0	2/0	3/0	3/0	4/0	4/0	4/0				
60	6	4	4	2	2	1	0	2/0	3/0	3/0	4/0	4/0	4/0						
70	6	4	2	2	1	0	2/0	3/0	3/0	4/0	4/0								
80	6	4	2	2	1	0	3/0	3/0	4/0	4/0									
90	4	2	2	1	0	2/0	3/0	4/0	4/0										
100	4	2	2	1	0	2/0	3/0	4/0											

24 volts

amps	10	15	20	25	30	40	50	60	70	80	90	100	110	120	130	140	150	160	170
5	18	18	18	16	16	14	12	12	12	10	10	10	10	10	8	8	8	8	8
10	18	16	14	12	12	10	10	10	8	8	8	6	6	6	6	6	6	6	6
15	16	14	12	12	10	8	8	6	6	6	6	6	4	4	4	4	4	4	2
20	14	12	10	10	10	8	6	6	6	6	4	4	4	4	2	2	2	2	2
25	12	12	10	10	8	6	6	6	4	4	4	4	2	2	2	2	2	2	1
30	12	10	10	8	8	6	6	4	4	4	2	2	2	2	1	1	1	1	1
40	10	10	8	6	6	6	4	4	2	2	2	2	1	1	1	0	0	0	2/0
50	10	8	6	6	6	4	4	2	2	2	1	1	0	0	0	2/0	2/0	2/0	3/0
60	10	8	6	6	4	4	2	2	1	1	0	0	0	2/0	2/0	3/0	3/0	3/0	3/0
70	8	6	6	4	4	2	2	1	1	0	0	2/0	2/0	3/0	3/0	3/0	4/0	4/0	4/0
80	8	6	6	4	4	2	2	1	0	0	2/0	2/0	3/0	3/0	3/0	4/0	4/0	4/0	4/0
90	8	6	4	4	2	2	1	0	0	2/0	2/0	3/0	3/0	4/0	4/0	4/0	4/0	4/0	
100	6	6	4	4	2	2	1	0	2/0	2/0	3/0	3/0	4/0	4/0	4/0				

32 volts

amps	10	15	20	25	30	40	50	60	70	80	90	100	110	120	130	140	150	160	170
5	18	18	18	18	16	16	14	14	12	12	12	12	10	10	10	10	10	10	8
10	18	16	16	14	14	12	12	10	10	10	8	8	8	8	8	6	6	6	6
15	16	14	14	12	12	10	10	8	8	8	6	6	6	6	6	6	4	4	4
20	16	14	12	12	10	10	8	8	6	6	6	6	6	4	4	4	4	4	2
25	14	12	12	10	10	8	8	6	6	6	6	4	4	4	4	2	2	2	2
30	14	12	10	10	8	8	6	6	6	4	4	4	4	2	2	2	1	1	1
40	12	10	10	8	8	6	6	4	4	4	2	2	2	2	1	1	1	1	1
50	12	10	8	8	6	6	4	4	2	2	2	2	2	1	1	0	0	0	0
60	10	8	8	6	6	4	4	2	2	2	2	1	1	0	0	0	2/0	2/0	2/0
70	10	8	6	6	6	4	4	2	2	1	1	0	0	0	2/0	2/0	2/0	3/0	3/0
80	10	8	6	6	4	4	2	2	1	1	0	0	0	2/0	2/0	3/0	3/0	3/0	3/0
90	8	6	6	6	4	2	2	2	1	0	0	2/0	2/0	2/0	3/0	3/0	3/0	4/0	4/0
100	8	6	6	4	4	2	2	1	0	0	2/0	2/0	2/0	3/0	3/0	3/0	4/0	4/0	4/0

(Wire sizes in AWG)

From *Boatowner's Mechanical and Electrical Manual,* by Nigel Calder (International Marine, 1990)

INDEX